LESSONS IN HUMOUR

SAYED ATHAR HUSAIN NAQVI

Published by New Generation Publishing in 2014

Copyright © Sayed Athar Husain Naqvi 2014

First Edition

The author asserts the moral right under the Copyright, Designs and Patents Act 1988 to be identified as the author of this work.

ISBN: 978-1-910053-42-3

All Rights reserved. No part of this publication may be reproduced, stored in a retrieval system or transmitted, in any form or by any means without the prior consent of the author, nor be otherwise circulated in any form of binding or cover other than that which it is published and without a similar condition being imposed on the subsequent purchaser.

www.newgeneration-publishing.com

 New Generation Publishing

In love of my grandchildren and the Momeneen - the righteous men who are my source of inspiration for writing this book.

Table of Contents

Acknowledgements	6
Preface	7
The Blanket is not leaving me	13
Now Tell Me Who Pushed Me?	15
Breaking the Onions on the Heads	18
Bunder-Baant – The Monkey Distribution	21
The Mound of Beauty	25
The Atheist and the Miracles	30
The Maharaja and the Manhoos	36
Janch Pardtal - the Investigation	40
The Horse, the Jew and the Prophet	43
Dave and Fred	48
The Laddoo and the Brahman	51
The Molvi and the Feast	56
Haandi Waali Majlis	59
The Great Abid	62
The Superman in Islam	71
The Reformer and the Taliban	75
The Taliban and the Jew	78
The Black Burqa and the Hijab	98
Khyali Pulau – Building Castles in the Air	106
Friends from the Facebook	112

Acknowledgements

I am thankful to my daughter-in-law, Sayeda Zaira Husain for editing this book.

And I am thankful to the Hadith:

Mezahul Momenina Aebadah

To humour a Momin is worship.

The clarity of this Hadith needs no words to be expended on its elaboration. Still its merits need to be expounded.

This amazing Hadith makes men move towards togetherness. And among other wonders of this Hadith, the minimum is, it gives impetus to cheerfulness, homogenises temperaments and is a great source of solicitation for prolonging life and owning loyalty of friends and keeping one's self in good humour.

My acknowledgements are due also to the strength of the Shia faith which filters my thought through the strainer of justice and reveres me rise to entertain Momeneen through adjudged humour, and emboldens me take stand to shield the society against the extremism.

Preface

The true nature of the people of a land will not be known unless the folk speech of the country-folk is studied and typical jokes of the folks in vogue are gone through. I am from among those descendants of the old school of the subcontinent of India of pre-modernity, now in London, who was brought up among the folks in India and has heard the storytellers - the old time literate among the illiterate. Their thoughts, catchwords and inflections, have been recollected by me and developed into entertaining stories.

These stories have lessons in ethics and mannerism, besides their entertaining values. The axioms in these stories are commonly used in light discussions to sum up a situation and for creating humour and laughter. An example of a commonly spoken catchword is:

Wahi Ghorda Wahi Maaidan.

The same horse, the same field.

This phrase immediately suggests that a person is talking of his or her everyday routine, but it shows wit and humour and is an amusing way of expressing a routine occupation. This phrase sheds light on the easy nature of the people, points to the content of humour in them and their easy mannerism. There is another phrase:

Ghorda Ghas say Pyar Karay Toe Kha-ay Kya?

If the horse starts loving grass then what he will eat?

This phrase teaches one to be practical and not emotional. It has also hidden mischief in it, but it is said in a charming way. There is another phrase:

Gadha Palo, Ghorda Palo, Khushfahmi Naheen Palo.

Rear ass, rear horse, but do not rear vain hope.

All this humour phrased by the people of India has no barrier of any ism and it is international property.

The rudiments of the folk stories collected by me have been developed and written with a fresh blend of thought and insight to cheer up the reader. These stories have ethical values, besides their entertaining values and will have their impact on the reader.

In addition to narrating these old time stories, I have developed some critical stories to focus on the extremism. The cause of the extremism is the impetuous interpretation of the religious beliefs and it is leading to terrorism. The less competent limited in understanding and less educated are easily misled and become tools of extremism and even its champions and turn to bigotry. But it is not entirely the lack of education that is making the terrorist emerge at the flash of light. It is also the deliberately falsified religiosity that is conditioning the emergence of a particular state of mind.

A Jamaat-e Islami young son, an engineer, graduating in 2008 from the Engineering University in Karachi was killed in Miramshah in North Waziristan camp of the Taliban by a drone attack on 29 November 2013. This was the result of the perversion of mind and not the lack of education that had made him a terrorist.

This young activist had turned a terrorist due to the extremism he inherited from his Jamaat-e Islami family and the motto of this political party, he followed. And take away the defective religiosity from the Pakistani terrorist what he follows - he is a good man - an extremely good man. But there is the general phobia in the people from non-adherence to the religiosity due to the extreme religiosity, and then the level of the religious knowledge is superficial and wanting. The only thing alleviating the ego of the common man in this God given land of Pakistan are the verses of poetry, which are the common heritage of the people if not immured by the religionists.

Koee Ho Ja-ay Musalman toe Dar Lagta Haai

Molvi Phir Na Bana Day Oosay Kafir Baba

Anwar Masood

If anyone becomes Muslim then fear hangs on me

Lest the Molvi makes him again Kafir, O dear friend

The extremism is spreading in Pakistan like the wild fire and with such a certainty as the sun rises in the east and sets in the west. This is a very serious ailment and it needs attention of all the nations of the world and their administering of an elixir for its cure. It is more serious a menace than the global warming taken up by our good Prince Charles, who says, climate change sceptics are 'headless chicken brigades'. But what catchword will be used to dampen the spirit of the terrorist, only a mind as fertile and nature as sweet as of Prince Charles can find.

The terrorists are turning regions in the world into wasteland. They are making people abandon their homes and hearths, who are migrating to safer places. There is no cure to the terrorism, save the use of the elixir of ethics to reform the mind. The terrorists cannot be herded in and locked up using physical means. This book will contribute to eliminate and simulate a cure to the extremism and bigotry. It is equipped with the sayings of the Prophet of God and the sayings of the Wali-e Azam – the highest friend of God, which are the dictations to the cure of the terrorism.

The word of the Prophet of God Hazrat Mohammad Mustufa SAWW, addressing the nation of Islam is:

Inni Tarikun Fikmurus-saqlain Kitab-Allahay Wa Itrati Aehlebaaiti.

I am leaving behind among you, two weighty things; the Book of God and my progenies, the Aehlebaait.

This Hadith is saying with its logical inference: 'as long as you will hold on to the two weighty things, you will not be lost'. This Hadith is the cure for the terrorism.

Then there is the Sermon no. 149 in the Nahjul Balagha of the Wali-e Azam, Ameerul Momeneen, Hazrat Ali Ibn-e Abi Talib A.S. - the first Imam from the Aehlebaait, which says:

Waqdamoo Alallah-e Mazloomina Wa Laa Taqdamoo Alaaihay Zalemeen

Go to God in the guise of an oppressed, not in the guise of an oppressor.

Hazrat Mohammad Mustufa SAWW, the fountainhead of all ethics and the God virtue has used for Hazrat Ali A.S. the title of Maula – the Lord, to whom every soul has to surrender his being. The Prophet SAWW says for him and Hazrat Ali:

Ana Madinatul Ilm-ay Wa Aliun Baboha

I am the city of knowledge and Ali is its gate.

This book is poised to quote the sayings of the great Prophet the humanity had its good fortune to behold, own and possess and it is poised to quote that great Wali, who is the totalities of all goodness and light in the world. And it is poised to tread the path of:

Amr Bil Maroof Wa Nahi Anal Munkir

The practicing of the renowned - the good deeds and withholding from the undesirable - the bad deeds.

Amr Bil Maroof Wa Nahi Anal Munkir are the fundamental ethical principles - the lifeblood of a healthy society. Their application is a *Wajoob* – a compulsion under the *Fiqhi* – jurisprudential principle of all the religions of the world – and they are a built in phenomenon in the nature and the sincerity of Islam.

The submissiveness and surrender to the *Wajoob* of the *Amr Bil Maroof Wa Nahi Anal Munkir* is to listen to and practice the sayings of the Messenger of God, Hazrat Mohammad Mustufa SAWW and to practice the sayings of the Wali of God, Ali-e Murtuza A.S. Their various sayings are numerously quoted to decorate this book and these will please the soul of the reader. Also occasionally quoted in the book are the sayings of the Imams of the House of the Prophet SAWW to further illuminate and beautify the book. The saying of the Prophet of God is:

Mezahul Momenina Aebadah

To please the heart of a Momin is worship.

In the same vein the saying of the Wali of God is:

'Jolliness and cheerfulness are the snares of friendship.'

Robert Louis Balfour Stevens, the Scottish novelist, poet, essayist and travel writer says:

'Man is a creature who lives not upon bread alone but principally by catchwords.'

The Reader Digest's catchword is 'Laughter is the best medicine.'

This book treads the foot prints of these spirited sayings. Humour does not seek philosophic acumen, but love, cheerful disposition and words selected to portray humour by the writer. This book does that and is poised to strike at the cord of humour and generate tenderness in the reader.

Wassalam,

Sayed Athar Husain Naqvi
    January, 2014

1

The Blanket is not leaving me

Two greedy mates were going down a river bank that one of them saw a blanket floating in the river. He said to his mate, 'Look there is a blanket floating in the river!' His mate looked at the blanket and said, 'It's a blanket all right.' He said, 'I'll go and get it.' The man jumped in the river and swam to the blanket and caught it. But he found it was not a blanket, it was a bear swimming in the river.

The man as soon as he realised it was not a blanket but a bear, left it quickly to get away from the thing and get out of the river. But the bear caught him and did not let him go. The man tried hard to be out of the hold of the bear. But the bear would just not let him go.

His friend at the bank wondered why his mate is taking so long. So he shouted from the bank, 'Have you got the blanket?'

The man in the river replied, 'Yes I have got the blanket.' 'Then what's taking you so long?' shouted his friend.

The man replied, 'I am returning, but this blanket is in my way.'

The man at the bank shouted, 'If the blanket is in your way, then leave the blanket and come back.'

The man in the river replied, 'I am leaving the blanket, but the blanket is not leaving me!'

Sayings of the Prophet of God, Hazrat Mohammad Mustufa SAWW:

Ad Dunya Darul Gharoor Wal Aakhera Darus-suroor.

The world is the place of deception and the hereafter is the place of delight.

Ad Dunya Mazratul Aakhera.

The world is the harvesting field for the hereafter.

Sayings of Hazrat Ali A.S.:

Remember well - today is the day of action, not of judgement, and tomorrow will be the day of judgement, not of action.

Make it incumbent upon thee to aim at attaining useful outcome and do not care for the results, they are beyond thy power.

However much the upheavals of the world harass thee, thou shouldst always look forward for happy days, which thou art sure to obtain eventually.

One who did *Amr Bil Maroof* – spreading and doing good deeds; he strengthened the back of the Momin and one who did *Nahi Anal Munkir* – stopping one from bad deeds; he disgraced the Kafir (the denier of God). He who has good-will is rewarded; he leads a cheerful life and is loved by others.

2

Now Tell Me Who Pushed Me?

A Sardar Sahib did not know how to swim. He was standing at a *Talaab* (a deep water swimming pool) and looking at the people swimming in the Talaab. A man started drowning in the Talaab and the people started shouting to save the man.

The people saw, the Sardar Sahib jumped in the Talaab. The Sardar Sahib when in the water started throwing his arms and feet to save him from drowning, as he did not know how to swim. The man who was drowning was kicked by the feet of the Sardar Sahib and pushed by his arms and he got to the bank safely. But the Sardar Sahib started drowning in the water.

When people saw that the Sardar Sahib is drowning in the water, they started shouting to save the Sardar sahib. A rescuer ran and jumped in the water and got the Sardar Sahib out of the water.

When the Sardar Sahib was out of the water, the people said to the Sardar Sahib, 'Sardar Sahib, you didn't know how to swim, yet you jumped in the water to save the drowning man, without caring that you will drown; how brave of you!'

The Sardar Sahib, who was already very angry at what had happened to him, got angrier at this poke at him and in a burst at them said:

'Bakwas Bund Karo, Yeh Batao Mujhay Dhakka Kisnay Diya Thha.'

'Don't talk rubbish; tell me who had pushed me?'

Dhakka Kisnay Diya is a maxim so often used in the subcontinent of India and the classic use of this maxim 'Dhakka Kisnay Diya' was made by the commentators in the case of General Pervez Musharraf. He was in the air, returning to Pakistan and his commercial plane was not allowed to land in Pakistan by the belligerency of the prime minister[1] who used constitutional power more for his false ego than for the service of the nation and there was the coup in its repercussion in 1999 and the General was pushed to take over in its wake.

But justice is multifaceted in Pakistan. A squint eyed chief justice, an Aaiby – defective in look and direful by nature was shoulder lifted to sit on the seat of the C.J and the General was gunned by his judicial infamy and pinned by that sullen prime minister with his dagger

---

[1] Mian Nawaz Sharif was Prime Minister; he attacked the Supreme Court of Pakistan. He set a set of judges against the Chief Justice of Pakistan, Syed Sajjad Ali Shah and split the Supreme Court of Pakistan in two parts, one in Quetta and one in Islamabad. The C.J. was removed in December 1997 through this manipulation, who was trying Mian Nawaz Sharif in contempt of court. He sent one Naval Chief home, one Chief of the Army staff home, both in 1999 and sacked the next Army Chief, General Pervez Musharraf in 1999 when he was returning home to his country, and appointed his yes-man general in his place. The army at this stage could not tolerate the intrigue any more, the Prime Minister was getting out of hand, damaging the army and violating the constitution and it staged a coup. General Pervez Musharraf was in the air and he was pushed to take over.

thrust in revenge and with his fire vomiting, rough of tongue PMLN workers at his back, the plot was complete and the General was dragged to the court for overthrowing this rash prime minister. The moral right of the coup by the army could not be challenged, but the absurdity of the arguments and the revenge mania of these politicians continued to tease the General.

Sayings of the Prophet of God, Hazrat Mohammad Mustufa SAWW:

God does not look at your (*Soorat aur Daulat*) appearance and wealth; He looks at your hearts.

One who does not give his thanks to the people; he cannot be thankful to God.

To treat the *Sael* - a beggar or a petitioner politely, is also included in the charity.

Sayings of Hazrat Ali A.S.:

The noble do not vindicate the mean, while the latter do not value the former.

A wise man is never tired of consultation. To take advice is the best way of self-help.

Many a base fellow has been made respectable and trust-worthy because of his wisdom, while many a respectable man has been rendered worthless because of his folly.

3

Breaking the Onions on the Heads

A king was famous for giving a better present to a gift presenter in return, when he was presented a gift. People came to the King to present their gift and receive back a better present from him. The news of the King's generous tradition reached to the far off places, to places beyond the limits of his country. Two Pathans lived in the mountains. They heard of the King's tradition and decided to go and present a gift to the king and receive a better present from him.

They went to the Bazaar - the market place to buy a nice present for the King. The best things in their country were the dry fruits. These grew abundantly in the mountains and were sold cheap there. A fruit merchant suggested to the Pathans to take two sacks of *Akhroat* (the walnuts) for the King, one sack each. He said it would be a nice present.

There were plenty of Akhroat in the country of the Pathans and were sold cheap. So the Pathans said to the fruit merchant, 'It is a cheap present, not worthy of gift to a King. We want to buy expensive present worthy of gift to a King.' And they went to the shopkeeper who had onions and bought two sacks of onions for the King.

The onions were expensive in their country, as these did not grow so much in the mountains. Each Pathan took one sack of the onions on his head and they carried the sacks to the King to offer to the King and be rewarded.

The Pathans travelled long distances day and night and at last reached to the capital of the king and went to the palace of the King with their present to get the reward and told the palace guards, 'we want to see the King to make a present to him.' Two guards went to the King and informed him that two Pathans have come from a faraway country and have brought two sacks of some rare present for him and they want an audience with him to present their gift.

The King showed his pleasure to give an audience to them. He ordered that the court be called. So the courtiers came and got seated in their regalia and the Pathans were led to the court. The Pathans turned up with their sacks of the onions on their heads.

The Pathans said to the King - 'We have brought expensive present from our country for your kingship. We expect your kingship will be pleased with our present.' And they opened the sacks of the onions.

When the king saw the Pathans have brought onions as present to him, he was very angry with the Pathans to have bothered him to hold the court and present onions. He was also angry with the Pathans, because they had put him in a dilemma as to what better present to give to the Pathans in return. The King thought long and at last spoke, 'break all the onions the Pathans have brought on their heads and afterwards ask them to clear off from my kingdom.'

The Pathans were seated on the floor and two warriors; one after the other started breaking the onions on the heads of the Pathans. When the onions were being broken on the heads of the Pathans, one Pathan said to the other:

'*Khoochah*, the King is not happy with our expensive present.'

The other Pathan said: '*Khoochah*, if the King is not happy with such expensive present as onions, he could never be happy with cheap Akhroat, the fruit merchant was suggesting.'

The first Pathan said, 'Khoochah thank God we didn't bring that cheap thing; we would have been treated much worse had we brought that to this mad King.'

Hadith of Hazrat Mohammad Mustufa SAWW:

Knowledge without practice is like cloud that has no rain.
Wealthy if not charitable is like a tree that has no fruit.
Beggar and indigent, if not showing patience, are like a river that has no water.
Young with no penitence is like a house without roof.
And woman that is impudent is like food that is without salt.

Sayings of Hazrat Ali A.S.:

Verily, he who depends entirely upon his own judgement and does not consider it necessary to consult others exposes him to dreads and dangers.
Patience is bravery, piety is wealth and abstinence is a shield.

4

Bunder-Baant – The Monkey Distribution

Two cats used to come to the house of an old lady. They used to come and kill the mice of her house and keep the house clean of the rodents. The old lady was very pleased with the cats and welcomed them in her house. The cats freely roamed in the house, toured the house and searched the mice and the old lady treated them like the blue-eyed children of the house.

One day the old lady gave some Helwa to the cats. The cats used to hover round the *Nemat Khana* – the cabinet with shelves in their spare time. The old lady kept Helwa and other delicacies in that Nemat Khana and the cats greedily smelled the delicacies. The old lady was generous and gave some Helwa to the cats. The cats were very pleased to get the Helwa.

The cats took the Helwa outside of the house to divide it between them. They made two portions of the Helwa and when they started to pick their shares one cat said to the other, 'Your share is bigger than mine.' The other one said, 'No your share is bigger than mine.' And in this way they started quarrelling with each other, saying that 'the share you are taking is more than half, and bigger than mine.'

They again made two halves of the Helwa and when again one took one portion, the other said, 'Your portion is bigger than mine', and like that they kept quarrelling over their shares.

They were quarrelling like that that a monkey came. He was watching their quarrel and said to them, 'The cats sometimes have problem between them and that's when the monkey comes to solve their problem.' The monkey said, 'You seem to be disagreeing on the shares of your Helwa? I will make the correct distribution of this Helwa between you two, so that you will not quarrel over it. Would you like me to do that?'

The cats liked the monkey's proposal and invited the monkey to make their shares. The monkey asked the cats to bring scales to weigh the Helwa to make the shares. The cats went in the house of the old lady and brought her small scales that the old lady used to weigh things on. They gave it to the monkey.

The monkey made two portions of the Helwa and put these on the scales, one portion on each pan and lifted the balance. One side of the Helwa was more than the other side and the pan tilted to that side. The monkey said, 'Oh! This side is heavier. I must not allow any excess given to either of you and see that each of you gets the Helwa not anymore than the other,' and he took some Helwa from the heavier side and ate it up.

After the monkey ate up the Helwa from the heavier pan, the Helwa on the other side became heavier and the scales tilted to that side. So the monkey took some Helwa from that heavier side and ate that up, saying, 'Now that side had more Helwa.'

By doing so the other pan became heavier and the scales tilted to that side. The monkey then took some Helwa from that side and ate that up, saying; 'Now this side was heavier,' and in this way he ate up all the Helwa.

The cats sat looking at the monkey and he was eating up all their Helwa. And the maxim evolved - Bunder-Baant or the monkey distribution. In this Bunder-Baant, the monkey had eaten up all the Helwa and the cats had got none.

The cats learnt after their Helwa was eaten up that it was better if they had settled the dispute between them themselves and had taken a little less and had not run after a little more.

There is an old Indian saying:

Aadhi Chhord Poori Ko Dhaway, Aadhi Rahay Na Poori Paway.

Leave half and run after the whole; leaves you getting neither the half nor the whole.

Sayings of the Prophet of God, Hazrat Mohammad SAWW:

The *Qewam* - the stability, of my religion is from four things:

1. From the learning of the scholars,
2. From the charity of the wealthy,
3. From the justice of the rulers,
4. And from the supplications of the beggars and the needy.

The Prophet SAWW said, 'three things are deadly':

1. Avarice indulged,
2. Passion pursued,
3. And self-conceit.

Sayings of Hazrat Ali A.S.:

He, who shows himself to be poor, always remains poor.

He, who has less avarice and greed, also has less which will drag him towards vices.

He, who fights and quarrels, it is difficult for him to retain fear of God.

He, who behaves cheerfully, is better than the benefactor who obliges harshly.

To be attributed with good qualities is nobleness, and to fulfil a promise is the sign of magnanimity.

5

The Mound of Beauty

The tradition and the mannerism of the Taliban[2] was that there should be no delay in the production of the offspring once a couple were married.

They looked into the marriage solemnization between Aishwarya Rai and Abhishek Bachchan. These celebrities became a wedded entity and that too, two years back in April 2007 and the Taliban found, no offspring were born to the couple so far. They decided that Abhishek Bachchan was breaking their rule of marriages, and also disobeying God's injunctions to produce and increase His children on earth. They concluded Abhishek was intellectually behind times, not seeing the philosophy of creation explained 1400 years back and not obeying God's rules and His purpose of pairing His creation into couples to increase their numbers.

Abhishek Bachchan was found guilty by them by their rule and also by God's edict and they decided to go to Bombay to catch this naturalised Aryan and straighten him up. They therefore sent a team of five raiders on 26th November 2008 to Bombay.

---

[2] The word Taliban includes all the *Zaili* or the subsidiary and the *Hamkhyal* or the similar thinking group of people, violating law. These people are extremist and bigot. They have names like Tahreek-e Taliban Pakistan, Lashkar-e Taiba, Jamat ud Dawa, Lashkr-e Jhangvi, Al Qaeda, in fact, in total sixty-two of them.

The team of the Taliban raided the sprawling city in ten different places to capture Abhishek Bachchan to do his *Shubhrata* (gleaming whiteness) and reverse-Shuddhi[3] to the standards of the Taliban thinking. But the team could not catch Abhishek, though they raided with a map in their hand to guide them and locate Abhishek and killed 160 people who came in their way.

The Indian security, out of panic, rather than catch the Taliban, killed all of them and they became dead like spent cartridges. Only one Taliban in this escapade, Ajmal Amir Qasab was caught by them. They overpowered this relative of the Punjab Taliban and the Taliban mission failed to catch Abhishek Bachchan. They met their *Naash Vinash* – total destruction.

The Taliban High Command however did not give up and decided to raid again and started preparation to make another hop from Karachi to Bombay to get this violator of God's edict, otherwise a rational and behaving Brahman of knowledge and of scrupulosity and of a look conducive to humour and intellectualism.

People should have sympathy with Abhishek Bachchan, but since the intention of the Taliban is sinister, Abhishek Bachchan must for the sake of peace in the world, shoulder his responsibility and discharge it like a friar and produce what the Taliban demand of him.

The cause of attack by the Taliban on Bombay is therefore no longer an unsolved mystery. The Taliban

---

[3] Shaardha Nand in India started a movement by the name of Shuddhi to make all the Muslims Hindu.

were after Abhishek Bachchan for not producing offspring and so, rather than he wanders around aimlessly in Bombay, Abhishek would do better to concentrate on the production of the offspring for the well-being of all.

He is seen randomly walking, coming and going with no apparent aim. In a film, a man drops a boulder on him from the roof-top considering him sacrificial soul to get him when he popped up at the targeted place and entered in a building below in a suspicious way. And he is advised not to invite any more trouble for himself and bury his difference with the Taliban by accepting them as his guide in marriage matters.

Lucky for Abhishek Bachchan, the Providence smiled and the good news spread one day on 23 June 2011 that Amitabh Bachchan was going to be grandfather. Aishwarya Rai and Abhishek Bachchan had a baby girl after four years on 16 November 2011 and the baby received world attention with congratulatory notes sent to the family from all quarters of the world. The Taliban's demand was met and all was fine between India and the Taliban. And the Taliban did not need their neck stuck out for their presence felt in India.

The Taliban therefore retired to the exclusivity of the messy affairs of the indecisive Pakistan. They withdrew to their home playground and intensified bomb blasting all over the land with a renewed vigour to hurry the demolition of Pakistan and start their rule on its ruins.

India was spared the terror from these promiscuous kings of terrorism, but Pakistan was gripped by their saturnalia of blood thirst especially to kill the Shias and the government in collusion with them began appeasing these ogres by calling them stakeholders. India however kept its guns trimmed to open hellfire to convince the Taliban of the Indian sovereignty over their lands, which was a better judgement vis-à-vis the terror handling of Pakistan. The terror handling was not possible with terrorists made the stakeholders, would comment the pious souls from their tombs and the graves.

The rise of the Taliban in Pakistan was due to their menace-potential in terror. And this was because they were given a *Maskan* - an abode in Pakistan. This was because a non-competency virus of straggling religiosity pervaded in Pakistan that poisoned the mind and the moral of the ruling as of the others. The worst affected are the Taliban dictated Punjab governments of the PMLN in the centre and in the largest province, and the PTI also holding a chunk. The Facebook critics are lampooning them with harsh ridicules and slighting them and they are swallowing insult and satire like the children's toffees.

Tyranny when it has the upper hand; it does injustice, nepotism, incarcerations, deportations and killings, and virtuousness when it has upper hand, does equal-distribution of wealth, liquidation of impropriety, implementation of justice and imbuing a culture of decency. An example of the past injustices undone by Hazrat Ali A.S. was:

Hazrat Ali returned the lands to the Muslims, gifted by Hazrat Usman to his favourite clan men, and said:

'By God, if I had come across such money which was spent on *Mehr* – love of women and the purchase of concubines, I would have retrieved that also.'

The Taliban and their co-faith were so lopsided in their religious beliefs that if they heard of this action taken by their Maula Ali against their iconic symbol of piety Hazrat Usman, they would declare Hazrat Ali non-Muslim (Maz Allah).

Sayings of Hazrat Mohammad Mustufa SAWW:

Al Muslimo Mun Salama Al Muslemoon Mun Yadhi Wa Lesaneh.

The Muslim is that from whose hand and tongue, the Muslim people remain safe.

The daughter is blessing and the son is a precious gift.

To deal with people with justice and to be helpful to the brothers in faith is better than all the deeds.

Sayings of Hazrat Ali A.S.:

To abstain from evil is good in itself.

The loss of the external eye is better than that of the internal one.

He who consults the wise takes advantage of their wisdom.

One would not be as familiar with the paths of the earth as I am familiar with the paths of the skies.

6

The Atheist and the Miracles

An atheist came to know of four miracles the Prophet of Islam, Hazrat Mohammad Mustufa SAWW performed:

1. The splitting of the moon in two halves.
2. The calling back of the sun for the *Ada* (on time) Namaz of Hazrat Ali A.S.
3. Going on ascend to the heavens in the night time – on Meraj and al-Asra and seeing signs of God, and God talking to him in the familiar voice of the Wali Ali. And in spite of the thousands of years of this journey at lightning speed, the Prophet SAWW returning to earth in no time.
4. Completing all assigned prophetic duties and delivering the God's creation listening to him from despondencies, ignorance and discord to enlightenment and teaching Wahdatul Wajood – the existential monism and leading them to self confidence. And God for these feats the Prophet achieved made him the Last Messenger.

The atheist said, 'The splitting of the moon in two halves and calling back the sun, and God opening the heavens for the Meraj of the Prophet were a recurrent tour de force (masterpiece) of Mohammad.

Mohammad was and he showed his miracle. If God was to which He would proclaim and announce that He was by enacting His tour de force then why He should not shy away and appear to be recognised. For an atheist seeing is to believe.

The atheist continued: The journey to heavens on Meraj will require that the heavenly bodies change course and time stop and gravity become naught. And this would be the primal and the foremost event, ever since after the creation of the universe. And all this unimaginable trickery cast by God will be to stunt the atheist and stall him in his belief that God was not absent – that He was.'

The atheist said, 'this tour de force, God staged to influence the mind of the atheist was possible because the atheists had no power of any God-related ism to intervene on their behalf and compete with the God will. And because they had no god with power and surveillance capacity to match these open galore of the displays of God ready to dwindle the atheist's belief, this was a non-event in the absence of any challenge to God and was a routine matter of no credit and consequence.'

The atheist said, 'this unchallenged supremacy of one up god-ship that God was displaying was unfair, particularly so, since the atheists were without revelations of any composed truth from any source to them. They were orphans in face of no comforting anecdotes coming to them from higher source than themselves and their kinds, and there was no competing between the infinitesimal time inflation and then thereafter evolution in the creation of the world and the 'Kun' or 'be' command of God. And so the miracles enacted by the Prophet on the behest of God, Whoever He was, were unchallengeable and near the atheists not a feat, since these were not reproducible reality, only verifiable.'

And to the geniality of God, idealising Mohammad and making him the last Messenger for the mankind and decorating him with the title of the *Rahmatulil Aalemeen*; the atheist said: 'This was due to Mohammad's personal spiritual ascendancies and his galore assets in issuing *Ahkam* or the edicts and his hereditary sovereignties in all virtues of kinds and the sovereignty's superiorities over the worlds, rather than to do with the Majesty of God.'

The atheist said, 'God, Whoever He was; only found it convenient to air these qualities of grace, compassion and vulnerability to kindnesses in Mohammad to highlight His quality of creation, perfectionism and obscuration which was showing His self-centrism.'

The atheist said, 'The highlighting of His perfectionism was aimed at subduing the atheist. And God Whoever He was, for His tricks on the atheists at variance with His laws, ruthlessly disarmed them in God understanding by sending them to their intellectual abyss, for which ultimately He was so rueful for His tricks that He withheld sending congruent prophets anymore and stopped sending Messengers altogether.'

On hearing that skirmish, battle and brawl to deny the existence of God - all formed of ghastly remarks, the believer ever had the audaciousness to hear about God, from the God denying atheist, he felt exasperated and incensed he said, 'The world's incongruent philosophers are bent on churning out, hosts and hosts of these heathenry atheists through lectures such as, 'man 3 - 5 billion years ago was a big carbon molecule.' As a consequence of these deaths to faith lectures, the religiosity is suffering and God's pervasive presence is being questioned.'

The believer said helplessly about the atheist looking at his being: 'You can't hold a slippery fish in your hand.'

The believer went on: 'God stopped sending Prophets, since His principles of justice and rule of law for the world with programme for the universe with causality and necessity as projected by Him were delivered in accordance with His intentions. But the atheists wanted to remain agnostic and call it, 'trick of God' and do not want to move away from their nihilism – the non-allegiance to anything of value.'

In reply to that mapping of the mind of an atheist, deficient from the viewpoint of the believer, the atheist said, 'I am just as broadminded a moralist as your great poet, litterateur and humanist, Asad Ullah Khan Ghalib.' And he quoted the poet's couplet:

Humko Maloom Haai Jannat Ki Haqeeqat Laikin
Dil Kay Bahlanay ko Ghalib Yeh Khyal Achcha Haai.

I know the reality of the Paradise, but (O friend)!
For entertaining the self, this thought is good.

On this unexpected assault by the atheist, the believer felt a degree cornered. But he swung the pendulum of his clock hard to flood the atheist with the elaborations of paradise. The believer said:

'Each individual, for his piety and his packages of good, taking them with him from the world after his soul departs from his carcass, has his level of Jannat in the paradise. There are assortments of Jannat and the entrants to it if joined hands with each other, together could make colonies of Jannat and share the expanses of its domains with each other, if all were harmonious with each other in their fundamentals of belief. In this happy situation their virtues could reach out to explore the vastness of the paradise and enter into any select Jannat they wanted to, like the migratory birds in the world seeking out congeniality.'

The atheist had no answer to such higher insight into the expanses of the paradise and the God relations. And only submitted ignorance about them and said, 'you are bound to go there from what I see in your tendencies in defending God. You are my colleague, if you take me to one of them there for long rest and appeasement, I am ready to go when you invite.'

This chapter came in existence, since I was talking to my philosopher colleague, Edward Hodgson of Pinner Philosophy Group, and I suggested something to him to which he replied he doesn't believe in God. This gave me the idea to write this chapter. Edward is welcome to Jannat if I am there for his smiling face and for the opportunity he gave me to express my belief.

Sayings of Hazrat Mohammad Mustufa SAWW:

Good bodings to him, who fears God instead of people, and instead of finding faults in the Momeneen, he is busy curing himself of his defects...

Pilgrims and visitants are emissaries and visitors of God. Great and Glorious is He. If they petition him He gives what they ask, if they seek His forgiveness He forgives them, if they call on Him, He answers, if they seek intercession it is granted.

The Prophet SAWW said, God will never accept repentance of any Bud Aekhlaq – bad mannered.

People asked O Prophet why it is so. The Prophet replied:

When he repents for one sin, then he does another bigger sin (because of his bad mannerism).

Sayings of Hazrat Ali A.S.:

Araft Allah Subhanahoo Be-fasakhatil Aza-ime Wa Hal Aqood.

I found out God the Glorified, from the resolves being broken and problems being solved.

Nothing can protect a kingdom as well as justice, while covetousness is the worst possible thing to incur God's displeasure.

O creatures of God! Fear God, adopt piety and with good deeds hasten to death, so that after death your name may be entered into the register of the pious and the virtuous.

7

The Maharaja and the Manhoos

There was a belief in India that if you started your day by seeing first thing in the morning the face of a cow then you were going to have a successful day. You were also going to have a successful day if you started the day by seeing first thing in the morning the face of a *Bhaag-waan* – a pleasant person. But if you started your day by seeing first thing in the morning the face of a *Manhoos* - an ill-starred or a wretched person, then the day was going to be a dreadful one for you.

A Maharaja believed in this maxim and understood it to be true. He was going on a hunting trip to the forest, the next day to shoot wild birds and hunt wild animals and enjoy the day there. He started early in the morning on the following day, but when he came out of his fort on an elephant for hunting, instead of seeing a cow, he saw the face of a man, who walked across the path of the Maharaja, showing his full face to the Maharaja.

A courtier accompanied the Maharaja in this hunting trip. The courtier was sitting behind the Maharaja in the *Haudaj* – the framework placed on the elephant. He said in the ear of the Maharaja to make him aware, 'Now your day is ruined; you have seen the face of this Manhoos first thing in the morning and now you will not get any game all day and it is going to be a bad day for you.'

The Maharaja became very angry with the man for showing his face to him and said to the palace attendants at the fort, the man was still walking across, 'take away the scoundrel and lock him up.'

When the Maharaja reached the forest, despite what the courtier had said, it turned out to be a very pleasant day for him in the forest. A serene breeze came to touch and tickle his face as he got near the forest. And then when he entered in the forest, it was as if the entire forest woke up to welcome him.

And when he reached to the heart of the forest, he found many game birds and wild animals; birds like: partridges, ducks, green pigeons, quail; and beasts like, leopard (Tendwa), boar (Jungli Suwar), and faunas like: wild goats, deer, and stag, all squeaking, squawking, singing, roaring and mewing, welcoming him and all offering them to be hunted down. The Maharaja was very pleased for seeing that man's face first thing in the morning. He was having such a wonderful day after seeing his face and he decided to reward the man for showing his face to him early in the morning.

When the Maharaja returned to his palace, he asked the palace attendants to bring that man, he ordered to be locked up. The Maharaja said, 'I want to reward him for showing his face to me first thing in the morning. After seeing his face first thing in the morning, I had such a successful day at the hunting.'

The man was brought to the Maharaja, but he was not looking at the Maharaja. He was walking slanting, leaning away from the Maharaja with his face turned away from the Maharaja and not looking at his face.

The Maharaja said to the man, 'What is the matter? You are not looking at my face. I was going to reward you for showing your face to me first thing in the morning. After seeing your face first thing in the morning I had such a successful day and got so many games to shoot in the forest.'

The man said to the Maharaja, 'Give whatever reward you like to give to me, but I am not going to look at your face. I looked at your face first thing in the morning and I was locked up all day!'

The Maharaj had gone for hunting with the apparent show of his intention and in a rig to do hunting and that was a fair deal. But if one went to hunt with a book in one hand and a stick in the other posing as a scholar and killed a pigeon with the stick which thought he was scholar and trusted him that was not fair. Or if one threw flash light in the eyes of the rabbit and blinded him and shot him dead that was not fair.

Sayings of the Prophet of God, Hazrat Mohammad Mustufa SAWW:

Love for the world is the root cause of all the evils.

A person who drinks water standing, and wears trousers standing or wraps turban sitting, God will land him in such trial and tribulations that has no cure.

Anyone who will remove the need of his fellow Muslim brother, God will meet his seventy-two needs in the hereafter.

The Prophet of God put an end to the exploitation of women by men. He gave them such status that never had they enjoyed before. The Prophet said:

'Paradise is under the feet of one's mother.'

Sayings of Hazrat Ali A.S.:

Men are not provided for in proportion to their wisdom, but they get provision in proportion to their lot. Had sustenance been taken by power, the hawks would have deprived the birds of prey of their food.

I have had the experience of the world for sixty years and never next to the religion, came across a thing better than selflessness, and never excepting infidelity, found a thing worse than beggary.

Truth is such a medicine which in taste is bitter, but in effect is sweet.

An old man's opinion is better than the young man's strength and vigour.

8

Janch Pardtal - the Investigation

A family had a marriageable-age girl and a proposal came to the family for the hand of this girl. The family members therefore in preparation of the marriage sent a member of the family to the town of the proposers to find out about the character of the man for whom the proposal had come to them from his guardians.

The family member went to the town of the proposers and located their neighbourhood. He then looked round for someone to ask about the character of this young man whose proposal had come to them and he found a man, whom he saluted and asked him, 'Do you know this man?'

The man said, 'Yes, I know this man.'

The man asked, 'What is the matter, why are you asking about him?'

The family member said, 'His guardians have sent his proposal for my niece and I have come to find out about the character of this man.'

The man said, 'Do you want to know in detail or in short about him?'

The family member said, 'In short please.'

The man said, 'There is nothing wrong with his character, his character is all right, only sometimes he lies.'

The family member was taken aback and said to the man, 'Did you say he lies?'

The man said, 'That only sometimes, when his mouth smells.'

The family member was astounded and asked the man, 'Did you say his mouth smells?'

The man said, 'That only now and then, sometimes when he eats onions.'

The family member was confounded and said, 'You said he eats onions[4]?'

The man said, 'That only now and then, when he takes *Chuski* - sips of Tharrda[5].'

The family member was shocked and said to the man, 'He takes Tharrda??'

The man said, 'That only now and then when he goes to *Mujra* - to the dance and song girl's *Adda* – the den.'

---

[4] The higher caste Hindu holy men do not eat onions for spiritual ascendancies. But the addicts of the Desi liquors take it raw to change the taste of their mouth.

[5] Tharrda is an intoxicating Desi drink, prepared from Mahuva - the sticky smelling sweet fruit from the Mahuva tree - a flourishing, thick, strong Indian tree.

Taardi is made from the palm tree. Its drunk smells from a distance. Small earthen pots (Haandis) are tied to the top of the tree trunk and an incision is made in the tree from which milk like liquid oozes out into the Haandi. The liquid is fermented and in time becomes highly intoxicating Taardi liquor.

The family member was horrified and said, 'He even goes to Mujras!'

The man said, 'He has only those habits otherwise he is all right, except that he is *Vela* - light of job and does nothing , only steals money of his family and squanders.'

The family member was revolted, he lost all euphoria to get his niece married, and said to the man, 'Thanks brother, you just stopped disaster entering in our house.'

Sayings of the Prophet of God, Hazrat Mohammad Mustufa SAWW:

God the Gracious never promotes ignorant and never disgraces a person who is equipped with learning.

The world is prison for the Momin and like paradise for the Kafir (the denier of God).

Sayings of Hazrat Ali A.S.:

Shake off thy indolence and lethargy, or thy continue lying in the abyss of obscurity.

I never found pleasure for the idle, but shame and despair.

If poverty enters from one door in the house of a Muslim, Islam goes out from the other door.

He who is ill-mannered is taken as an enemy, even by his friends and companions.

He who consults the wise takes advantage of their wisdom.

9

The Horse, the Jew and the Prophet

The Messenger of God, Hazrat Mohammad Mustufa SAWW was returning to Medina one morning, coming from its outskirts. It was a market day. A Jew joined in and began walking in front of the Prophet. The Jew was carrying a beautiful horse. The Prophet liked the horse and asked the Jew if he would sell the horse. The Jew said yes, he is taking the horse to the market place for selling it. The Prophet asked him how much he would sell it for. The Jew said 10 Dinars.

The Prophet bargained with the Jew and the price of the horse was settled at 9 Dinars. The Prophet said, 'All right I have bought the horse; you deliver the horse at the mosque and collect your payment there.' The Jew agreed. He was happy that the business of the day was over early and he will have the day free for himself.

Everyone knew where the mosque was and where the Prophet lived. The Jew walked at a brisk pace with his horse and when he got nearer to the market, he found more and more people were interested in his horse. People started putting price for the horse. If one would put one price, someone else would put a higher price than the previous one. First the Jew said no to the people in the market, but as the price got higher and higher, he changed his mind and decided to sell the horse to the highest bidder.

There was a crowd of people where the Jew was standing with his horse. By this time the Prophet also arrived there, where the Jew was. The Prophet saw some people whom he recognised. Many of them were Muslims and the Jew was selling the horse to one person in the crowed.

Just when the Jew was selling the horse, the Prophet had arrived and said to the Jew, 'Wait what are you doing with my horse, I have bought this horse from you and you are supposed to deliver the horse at the mosque and collect your money from there.'

The Jew said, 'No, I have still not sold the horse to you, the horse is mine and I am selling it for 15 Dinars to this customer.'

The Prophet said, 'But you cannot do that; the horse is mine. I have bought the horse from you!'

The Jew said, 'All right, if you have bought the horse then have you any witness to say that you have bought the horse?'

The Prophet had no witness, as there was no one outside of Medina where the deal had taken place between him and the Jew. The Prophet therefore was quiet. However of the many Muslims standing there, the Prophet asked them, 'Will anyone of you like to be my witness that I have bought the horse from the Jew?'

They said, 'O Prophet, how can we do this felony, we were not there, and how can we say whether you bought the horse or not.'

In this period, Zaid Bin Thabit came to that place and saw lots of people there, also that the Prophet SAWW is standing among them. When he enquired about the matter the Prophet said, 'I bought this horse from the

Jew and he is saying if you have bought the horse then bring a witness and there is no witness to this transaction.'

Zaid said, 'O Prophet of God! I am your witness that you have bought the horse.'

The Jew became quiet now when a witness came, but the Prophet said to Zaid, 'But Zaid, you were not present there, where our transaction went through, so how can you say that you are my witness?'

Zaid said, 'O Prophet SAWW! Everything you said about God that He is One, I became your witness, you said there is a hereafter, I became your witness, therefore, if you say you bought this horse, I become your witness.'

Hadith-e Qudsi - word of God through the tongue of the Holy Prophets. God says:

Faaz Karoni Az-kro Kum

You remember Me, I will remember you.

God said in Aayet 3: 144 of the Holy Quran:

God will definitely reward those who serve Him with gratitude.

Sayings of the Prophet of God, Hazrat Mohammad Mustufa SAWW:

Qala Sallallahoo Aelaihe Wa Aalehee, Sallemoo Alal Yahood Wal Nesara wa La Taslemoo Yahood Ummati.

Faqala Ya Rasool Allah Mun Yahood Ummatak, Qala Lazeena Yasma-oonal Azaan Wal Aeqama Wa La Yahzaroonal Jamaa-a.

So spoke (the Prophet), salutes of God be on him and on his family, do make Salam on Yahood and Nasaara, but do not send Salam on the Yahood of my Ummat.

People asked, 'Ya Rasool Allah who are the Yahood of your Ummat?' (The Prophet SAWW) replied, those, who hear Azaan and Aeqamat and do not join the congregation.

The Prophet said, offer prayer in any Masjid but not in the Masjid of a *Zalim* – a tyrant, running a *Firqawar* – sectarian mosque (Quote by Maulana Kalb-e Sadiq).

Sayings of Hazrat Ali A.S.:

A person who is of smooth politeness, his first advantage is that all people will be his helper if he is in confrontation with the ignorant.

Success is certain to come to the patient, be it takes a long time.

We prefer moderation: neither too much nor too little.

Excerpt from The Psalms of Islam – the prayer of the obedient to God:

O God! Inspire us to obey Thee

Turn us aside from disobeying Thee

Make it easy for us to reach the seeking of Thy pleasure which we wish,

Set us down in the midst of Thy Gardens...

(Presented here are 4 of the 28 verses of the Munajat - the supplications. These supplications are the inspirational works of the 4th Imam Ali A.S. - Zayn al-Abedeen - adornment of the worshippers. This Imam on the maternal side is grandson of the Sassanid Emperor Yazdgard III. He is Great grandson of the Prophet SAWW, Grandson of Hazrat Ali A.S. and Janab Fatima SUA and Son of Imam Husain A.S.)

Man loves his self and his love for himself increases with his increased obedience to God, since it brings in him increased piety and self satisfaction. His faith in himself increases and he greets his self and takes pride in his conscious. The Psalms of Islam are the operational manual and the pious and effective Hikmat – the God approved means which are that high that they are at the stage of Asmat – king of virtuousness and they invoke humility and piety in the supplicant.

10

Dave and Fred

There were two friends, Dave and Fred. Fred was slow and Dave clever.

Fred said to Dave, 'Dave! I went to the fields and saw at one corner of the field, she was standing there. '

Dave said, 'Oh yes, was she? What did she want?'

Fred said, 'Dave! She aimed at something, but I did not know what? At the other corner, her kids were standing, looking away from me.'

Dave said, 'Really! I wonder what she wanted with her kids there.'

Fred said, 'Dave! I never knew what she wanted; she looked so harmless and stood there looking at me.'

Dave said, 'Strange! Go on, what happened then?'

Fred said, 'Dave! I told her move off, but she stood there and nodded me.'

Dave smelled foul, and said, 'I see! Tell me then, what happened?'

Fred said, 'Dave! I went to her in a jiffy, and said move off, and she said, Mein, Mein, Mein, Mein.'

Dave said, 'She said, Mein, Mein, Mein; Mein! She was a goat you clot.'

Fred said, 'Yes Dave! That's what I was trying to tell you.'

Dave said, 'You took a hell of a long time to get that off your chest, you twit!'

Qalallah: God Exalted said:

Laelaha Illallah - There is no god but God:

(This secret in the wisdom) Is My strong fort, one who entered in it, he escaped My torment and entered in refuge.

The sayings of the Prophet of God, Hazrat Mohammad Mustufa SAWW:

A person who torments a Momin without any sin, it is, as though he demolished the House of Kaaba and Medina and the Baitul Mamoor (the prototype of Kaaba in the heavens).

The Prophet of God in his last sermon said:

Good bodings to those, whose Aekhlaq – manners is good, Khaslat – the nature is vice free, whose Batin – the interior is virtuous, the Zahir – the open is good, who spends his excess wealth in the way of God, but he be not Batooni – bombastic and from his side does justice with the people.

Hazrat Imam Hasan A.S. was such a graceful personality that he was an acknowledged manifest of virtues by friends and foe alike; justice, piousness, pieties and benevolence were his simple nature. This Imam says to explain of Faqr i.e. contentment – which stands not to show Zillat or indignity and not to be down trodden. This was the spirit of Islam induced by the Imam. The Imam said:

Do not ask for something from someone, even if it is to ask the way to a place.

Sayings of Hazrat Ali A.S.:

One, who makes haste in endeavours, becomes successful, while he who keeps hesitating is deprived.

Patience is a shield against all misfortunate happenings, while lamentation adds to miseries.

The endurance of troubles and difficulties makes a man great.

One's honour and dignity is not perfect, unless he carries others' burden and treats them kindly.

You should conceal your three things:

1. Power

2. Knowledge

3. Wealth.

No enemy can be satisfied, but with their destruction, because people in general are enemies to them.

11

The Laddoo and the Brahman

A Brahman - one Gyani – the one who gives Gyan or Knowledge to others, gave a big feast for his *Nirapad* and *Mukti* - freedom from misfortune and release from rebirth. He invited lots of Brahmans so that they will eat and pray for him that he may obtain peace in life in this world and salvation in the life of the hereafter.

The news of the feast reached to distant Brahmans and Brahmans from far and near started preparation to go to the feast. They started emptying their bellies over the number of days left ahead of the feast, eating scanty food over these days and preparing them to eat as much as they could eat at the feast.

On the day of the feast the Brahmans came in scores, and the host Brahman started feeding them with Puri, Kachauris, Bhaji and accompaniments of Achaar and curd in the Bhoj on fresh banana leave plates. And the Brahmans started filling themselves with the Bhoj.

The custom at the feasts was that the host Brahman fed to the guest Brahmans as much food as they could eat; so much so that the guest Brahmans exhausted themselves and became motionless with the load of the food in their bellies. And then in the end, the host Brahman offered Laddoo(s), and he picked a guest Brahman to entice him again and again to eat more and more and at each extra Laddoo the guest Brahman ate on his full belly, the host Brahman gave him one rupee for his greater guarantee to salvation and for the end Mukti or Moksha in the hereafter. And it was a great Punn (a holy act) to feed a hungry Brahman.

One Brahman had eaten too much, so much so in the Bhoj to his fill that he was motionless. He was full to the brim, but still when enticed with a Laddoo, he ate the Laddoo and collected a rupee and he ate so many Laddoo(s) that he fainted and then started to die.

The host Brahman, when he saw that his guest Brahman was dying eating his food, he called out loud and begged God, 'Hey Eeshwar! Hey Parm-aatma! Hey Bhagwan! Save this Brahman. If the life of this Brahman is saved, I will feed seven Brahmans in gratitude to You to their fill.'

Since God always listens to talks and grants requests when it is attached with charity, the Brahman was sure his prayer will be granted. The host Brahman therefore immediately started counting names of seven Brahmans whom he was going to feed. He had counted up to six Brahmans when the dying Brahman raised his finger and said, 'Don't forget to count me in the seven Brahmans.'

The Holy Quran taught that the easiest way to Mukti is the recitation of the Aayet, 21:87:

Laa - ilaaha Illaa Anta Subhaanaka Inni Kuntu Minaz Zaalimeen.

There is no God save Thee - Thou art the glorified! Without doubt I have been a wrong-doer.

God the Gracious sent the following revelation to Prophet, Hazrat Dawood A.S.:

O Dawood! There is no servant of Mine, who if instead of turning to *Makhlooq* (the creation), if turns his self to Me that I will not know of his request! Then if the sky and the earth do deceit and do scheming against him, I will Myself create road for his salvation.

God the Gracious spoke to Hazrat Moosa A.S.:

O Moosa! Any person who spends from his earnings in My way, then whatever he spends I give him ten times of it in this world and ninety times of it in the hereafter.

Ahadith of the Prophet of God, Hazrat Mohammad Mustufa SAWW:

One who will honour guest, though he is Kafir (a denier of God), on the day of the judgement, God will respect him.

O God! Forgive the pilgrim and those for whom the pilgrim seeks forgiveness.

Sayings of Hazrat Ali A.S.:

To eat a little, leads both to respect and to good health.

Riazatun Nafs — the exercise for the strengthening of the soul:

Never eat when you do not feel hunger.

If you do, you will get dullness of mind.

When you eat, eat Halal (that earned through honesty).

When you eat, take first the name of God.

These evils in the following five persons are extremely deplorable:

    1. Villainy in scholars.
    2. Avarice in philosophers
    3. Miserliness in rich men.
    4. Immodesty in women
    5. Adultery in old folks.

Many a base fellows have been made respectable and trustworthy because of their wisdom, while many a respectable men have been rendered worthless because of their folly.

These were the early days of Maula Ali's apparent Khilafat. Two companions, Talha and Zubair visited him to discuss a matter. They demanded from him to give them a counsel. Hazrat Ali A.S. asked them if it was a private matter or a state matter. They said it was a private matter.

At that time Hazrat Ali was working in the treasury. He was taking account of the Baitul Maal income and expenditure. There were two lamps burning to give light. He put out one lamp and asked them to proceed with the matter they have brought to discuss. They said, 'Ya Ali would it have been that we would share more light from that lamp you have put out or is it for our disdain that you extinguished it.'

Hazrat Ali replied, 'I have put out the other lamp as that one is state Property, run from state funding. The State is paying its running expenditure. And because you are going to discuss a private matter I have left my own lamp on, which is run by my expenses.'

Do not make haste in the performance of deed before time. Nor give it up when the favourable circumstances have come into existence. Nor turn to the evil and vicious things. Nor ignore them when they have come to light. Do everything in time.

12

The Molvi and the Feast

A Molvi Sahib was invited to a local wedding. The custom at these weddings was that a feast was served after the *Nikah* – the solemnization of the matrimony. So the Molvi Sahib did all the preparation for the feast by keeping his appetite sharp. He went there on the wedding day and took one pupil with him from the Madrasa as his *Baghalchap* – an extra person to walk alongside and give him help, and also to help himself in the feast.

Lavish food was served after the wedding ceremonies were over. The *Dastarkhwan* – the cloth spread sheet for laying food was filled with food and the feast started. The Molvi Sahib noticed his pupil is busy taking the food, but he is also so very often taking sips of water during the food. The pupil was sitting opposite the Molvi Sahib and the pupil took water after every few morsels of food. He took everything, chicken, Taftan, Nan, Pulau, Feerni and all the things present, but took sips of water after each few morsels of food.

When the feast was over, the pupil and the Molvi Sahib returned to the Madrasa. There the Molvi Sahib gave one slap on the cheek of the pupil and said, 'When the time to fill up with food had come, you were filling yourself with water.'

The pupil said to the Molvi Sahib, 'I was not filling myself with water, I was taking sips of water to press the layers of the food I had put in the stomach, so that I could take more food.'

The Molvi Sahib gave another slap on the cheek of the pupil and said, 'Why didn't you tell me this before?'

The Prophet of Islam, Hazrat Mohammad Mustufa SAWW one day so spoke to his companions:

Show forbearance over things you dislike. There is exceeding goodness in showing patience; and remember; success and victory is with endurance, and solace and ease is with hardship and hard work. Indeed after every hardship there is comfort.

The Prophet of Islam, one day so spoke about the interpretation of the Quran:

One who does exegesis of the Quran by his notional opinion, he be assured to have made his place in the hell.

Sayings of Hazrat Ali A.S.:

He, who cannot manage his affairs properly and gives them up; is indolent (lazy and lethargic), he is visited by troubles and difficulties, which come to awaken him.

Idleness produces not only childish and sprightly thoughts in one's mind, but a love for opposing others.

To do good to men, to help the poor and to feed guests are the signs of nobleness and leadership.

Make efforts and be not idle and give up indifference, as an idle man has to meet with shame, at last.

He who is not corrected by respect is righted by disgrace.

The sayings of the fourteen infallible Imams of Islam are the precious Jewels of the Shia faith. The Afaal-o-Aeqdar – the deeds and values taught by Imam Baqar A.S. are:

A person who does Ghussa and Ghazab - rage and wrath, he will never get comfort, till he enters in hell. A person, who is making rage on his people, if he is standing, should sit down, because doing this will remove the effect of the devil. And a person who becomes angry with his kind hearted relatives, he should get near them and touch them. Since by touching the kind hearted, one gets peace.

For 1400 years Islam graces the world with the affluence of justice. The greatest force of the moral ascendancy of the followers of Islam is *Adl* – the justice. The infallible Imams of the house of the Prophet SAWW have placed justice in the fundamentals of the faith as a separate element, though it is contained in the Wahdaniat – the Oneness of God.

13

Haandi Waali Majlis

A Lukhnawi used to go to a Majlis every year which a Nawab held at his Haveli or mansion. Every year a *Feerni Ki Haandi* (a clay pot filled with rice pudding) was distributed to the *Azadaar* - the mourners as their Majlis gift or *Tabarruk* or ex voto, at the end of the Majlis. The Majlis for that reason had gotten the name of 'Haandi Wali Majlis'.

The Lukhnawi each year used to go to the Majlis to get the Haandi. For many years it was all right. Then one year he felt that the Haandi was carrying a smaller quantity of Feerni than last year. He however took the Haandi and went home.

But next year when he went there, he was watchful about the quantity of the Feerni in the Haandi and when he was given the Haandi, what he found was that the Haandi was still the same size as before, but the Feerni was now even smaller than the last year. He was now convinced the Feerni was being pinched by someone and started shouting:

Aetni Bardi Haandi Aur Aetni Si Kheer, Ghaban Haai, Ghaban Haai, Ghaban!

Such a big Haandi and such a small quantity of Feerni, this is embezzlement, this is embezzlement, embezzlement.

There is a proverb in India:

Daan Ki Bachhiya kay Daant Naheen Gintay.

One does not count the teeth of the calf given in gift.

But the Majlis gift was different. The Haandi of the Majlis was not a *Daan* or donation, but a *Tabarruk* – a serving or ex voto. And this gift had a different nature and legitimacy phenomenon. The Lukhnawi's right to the Haandi was shielded and automatic. The Haandi was distributed in the name of the Sayyadush - Shuhada Imam Husain A.S. whose relationship with each Majlis comer was personal. So the Lukhnawi had an approved right to protest over the short Tabarruk.

Sayings of the Prophet of God, Hazrat Mohammad Mustufa SAWW:

Khaslatainay La Yajmaan-ay Fil Momin Al-Bukhl Wa Soo-al Khulq.

The characteristics of miserliness and the rudeness do not accumulate in a Momin, at once.

When you are taken over by anger, be quite.

Speaking truth leads to salvation.

Sayings of Hazrat Ali A.S.:

Take care not to turn your back upon a relative when you find him in starvation.

No legacy is better than good character, and no beauty is better than nobleness.

A wise man should spend his time to improve his livelihood, meditate upon his spiritual matters and to enjoy legitimate pleasures.

The Holy Quran in Aayet 5:55 identifies a Wali - identifies Ameerul Momeneen Hazrat Ali Ibn Abi Talib A.S., who gave his ring to the indigent calling for alms, while he was in Ruku. The words of the Aayet said:

Only God is your Wali (real friend) and His Apostle and those who believe. Who perform prayer and pay alms while they bow (in prayer).

God was just and fair and did not hold back praise for an act which was unusual. Ali was that perceiving creation of God who was filled with the manifests of God. Hazrat Ali was in pain. An arrow was pierced in his calf that could not be pulled out for pain. The Prophet said, pull out the arrow when Ali is in prayer.

Teeray Pewast Khaainch Lo Bola Nabi Nein

Ali Jab Mahway Surat Hoan Wahi Mein

Sayed Athar Husain

The arrow was pulled out when Hazrat Ali was in prayer and he was so engrossed in the prayer that he had no pain.

And in Ruku, he A.S. had knowledge and ears fixed at the call of the pleader seeking alms in the mosque and extended his finger to the Sael – the petitioner to take away the ring in alms. This Hamageeri – the overall control on senses was only possible in a Wali of Hazrat Ali's stature (who are Allah, Mohammad, Ali himself).

14

The Great Abid

There were three classes of people who fell under the phenomenology of worship and qualified them to be known as worshippers – one offering submission and devotion to God, and in exchange qualifying themselves to receiving reward[6] from God. However the worship was that summary act, in which each endeavour of the worshipper was a separate art in devotion and submission, which qualified the worshipper to be enlisted for acceptation in God's pleasure to its specified degree of recognition.

The list of the grade of the worshippers was great, however the phenomenology of worship and the reward grade from God created the following three major worshipers who strived in worship with their

---

[6] The worshippers of God exchanged their voluntarism with reward of benefaction from God. They became un-smirched in the world of the Aab-o Gil – water and soil, for their worship. Besides that they received the reward of the distinctive position in the paradise in the heavens, and respect accorded to them from God SWT (Subhanahoo Wa Tala) in the material world - the earth and it's environ. The beauty of the worship was that when the soul of the worshipper flew after the bondage with the body was broken, it was warmly welcomed by the environment where its creation took place, billions of years ago in the vicinities of the paradise, but it stood in waiting in limbo till the appointed day appeared when God in His Magnanimity and Majesty awarded the judgement for the grade to be awarded to the soul.

separate methods. These three classes of the worshipers were:

Abid – He transformed himself into a worshipping soul and attuned his mind to pure worship, un-distracted by the need and the requirements to furbish him with the phenomenology of seeking knowledge.

Zahid – He had his eyes fixed, body and soul on the hereafter and did everything right, and he possessed nothing in the material world, and knowledge pervade in him through the open eyed observation of his surroundings.

Arif – He was a knowledgeable soul and had read and absorbed the message from the great book of supplication and prayer - Sahifa-e Sajjadia (The Psalms of Islam, see p. 47) and had his mental efficacies in harmony with the Sahifa. His conscious was aroused to a level, where he understood the Oneness of God, and as Arif knew what Aebadat - the worship was, and what he was doing.

The Arif was a rock of a character an affronter to fallacies. He possessed an inquisitive mind and had found answers to questions pertaining to the models of truth, leading to God. And he had found answers to questions through the realm of monotheism and mysticism and had unearthed realities. His achievement aroused an aura of mystique about him, because he had recognised his Imam of the time appointed by God SWT on him, to whose grace and sublimity he saluted, after every Namaz every day, knowing that the Imam AFS was present and living[7].

One person entered in the phenomenology of worship and developed a great love and habit for doing *Aebadat* or worship. He would go to the mosque and start praying there incessantly. Day and night he prayed there, standing up for Namaz, and he doing his acts of worship.

This person became very famous as Abid. Prayer became his habit and fancy, and he gave up family and friends and set himself just to pray. Anyone in the town could tell who the Abid in the town was, and what his address was.

The news of his Aebadat reached to the Devil. The Devil was Iblees, Azazeel or Lucifer. He came to know that a man in the town has become very famous as Abid, because he is praying all the time and he has become a habitual Abid. Now the Devil was the original Abid. He had done prostration to God for thirty thousand years - 6 thousand years at each site,

---

[7] All the evidential circumstances show, Imam Mehdi A.S., the Twelfth Imam of the House of the Prophet of God, Hazrat Mohammad SAWW is living for the last 1200 years. His birth date is known but his death has not occurred to have been recorded. But his AFS's life is indefinite. He will appear, live to righting things and die. He AFS is alive now and Imam of the age for the mankind. He comes to help the needy, if he is called by the needy.

As to his presence being not see-able, it is not an enigma or occultation – it is a spirituality spell. It is the same; as the Prophet of Islam, Hazrat Mohammad SAWW was not able to be seen when he walked through the enemy cordon of forty men at the time of the Hijrat or migration. He was invisible to them - the enemies, who all had surrounded his house to kill him.

first on earth, then in each of the strata of the skies - first sky, second sky, third sky and so on, progressing to the fourth sky as he got promoted to these prestigious positions for his intensive prostrations. And then he got so big that he started lecturing to the angels.

And there was no one a bigger Abid than Iblees. But he was kicked out from the presence of God, because he was not an Aarif to see beyond his myopic sight and enter into the depths of knowledge and recognise his Imam (Hazrat Adam A.S.) – the Imam of the age.

And for that shortage in virtue of not being an Aarif, the Devil refused to do *Sajda* or prostration to other than God. All the angels prostrated to Hazrat Adam A.S. when God asked them, but Iblees refused God to bow to Hazrat Adam A.S., when God asked him to prostrate to Adam A.S. after He SWT blew His spirit in the clay-form of Hazrat Adam A.S., which He had created out of His will from the soil ordered brought to Him from earth. And for that disobedience, the Devil was kicked out from the presence of God and from all the vicinities of the heaven.

And since that time the Devil in vengeance[8] of Hazrat Adam A.S., whom he considered cause of his demise,

---

[8] The Devil was thrown out of the heaven, though he was a Malak, one made of fire. His problem was ego. Passion had let the devil down. And mankind – the descendant of Adam A.S. was made of earth. His problem was Jinsi – the sexual pull, and woman had let him down, but man had Zerf – capacity to submit his self and beseech for forgiveness from God (see history and origin of Adam A.S. elsewhere). However the Devil did not have that virtue to ask for forgiveness from God and he had become LUA - the accursed.

begged leave of God to sit astride across the right path of the progenies of Adam A.S. and fill evil in the willing of them and misguide the poorly equipped descendants of Adam A.S. and despoil their virtue of piety and piousness and in general create dark forces on the earth.

Jealousy took over the Devil, when he heard of the Abid, and his ego could not accept that the distinctive appellation of the Abid should fall into someone else's lap. The Devil said to himself, this Abid must be misled and weaned away from what he was doing.

He took the form of a revered person with a long beard and wore a white robe and went to the mosque and set himself to pray where the Abid prayed, near to the Mehrab – the niche in the mosque - the place for the Imam.

The Devil took position to the right side of the Abid and started to pray. He made one *Ruku* (bowing) after another and did one *Sajda* (prostration) after another and continued to pray non-stop.

The Abid saw that someone on his right side is praying non-stop and not stopping to take a break to eat and drink and go for needs. He immediately became very impressed by this Namazi and decided to ask him the secret of his long, non-stop prayer. He waited each time for the Devil to say his *Salaam* (salutation) at the end of his prayer to ask him the secret of his non-stop prayer, which was of seeming no end.

Every time the Devil said the Salaam and finished the set of the prayer he was going through that he immediately made a fresh *Niyat* by saying Allah-ho-

Akbar and started the new set of the prayer. The Abid every time lost the chance to ask him that how he could do the long non-stop prayer. He waited again and again for the end of the Devil's Namaz, but when it ended the Devil immediately stood up for the next set of prayer and said Allah-ho-Akbar. In this way the Devil never gave the Abid a chance to ask him of his secret.

The Devil was master in misleading and expert at generating spiritual imperfection in men and he was keeping an eye on the Abid during his planted Namaz, and when he saw he had aroused sufficient impatience in the Abid and he was now soft; at the end of the next Namaz, he said to the Abid, 'What did you want?'

The Abid was very obliged to the Devil to give him the opportunity to ask him the question about the secret of his long continuous Namaz and he said to the Devil, 'What I want to know is that how you are doing that? I see you are continuously praying and not stopping at all; I cannot do that.'

The Devil gave the short and curt reply to the Abid, 'That thing is not in you.' And he again said Allah-ho-Akbar and started his fresh set of prayer.

The Abid when he came to know that something was not in him, became anxious to know what it was that was not in him and he fixed his attention on each *Rukn* (the prayer stages) of the Devil, looking for a break in the Devil's Namaz to ask him the question 'what thing was not in him'. But the Devil fixed his acts not to give opportunity to the Abid to let him ask, and he kept the Abid waiting and not making any break in his Namaz.

After some time when the Devil saw, he had aroused sufficient impatience in the Abid, and the Abid was sufficiently softened, he paused for a moment and quickly the Abid shot the question at him what he had not in him?

But then again the Devil had said Allah-ho-Akbar for his next set of prayer. The Abid again was demoted to wait to know of the secret to reach to the level of the Devil in Aebadat, and at last when he found a gap in the Devil's Namaz, the Abid shot the question at the Devil, 'What have I not in me.'

The Devil saw the Abid was now absolutely down with passion, so he said, 'You don't have the element of sin in you and that is why you cannot pray the way I do.'

The Devil said, 'It is the fear of the penalty of sin that is driving me to pray like I do, so that God may notice and have mercy on me one day, and I may be forgiven without asking Him.'

The Abid, who was very fond of praying, was very thankful to the Devil to tell him that it was the sin that was making him pray like that. And it was sin that brought salvation without asking – only the remedy was prayer. But sin was a field the Aabid had not played in and he did not know what to do about the sin. The Abid had therefore to ask the Devil.

The Abid waited for the end of the next set of the Devil's Namaz to know what to do about the sin. And as soon as the Devil had said Salaam, the Abid let flow his feelings and poured out the trickles of his innocent mind, and what he had in his heart to the Devil. The Abid said to the Devil:

'I want to pray just the whole lot like you all the time. Please tell me how to enter in sin to reach to that degree of prayer you have entered in.'

The Devil was master of making falcon like attack on his prey and was waiting for that impromptu blurted out of the Abid's orifice. He said to the Abid, 'Go to the east corner of the town, there is this woman, you can pay her and do the sin and come back to start praying. You will be praying like me in fear of the sin and for forgiveness.'

The Abid who was just an Abid and not an Aarif, not knowing the purpose of praying and not carrying the knowledge of the quality of God to Whom he prayed, and was not following the infallibles and the lions of the house of the Prophet of God to assimilate the secrets of God, started his journey towards the sin to be able to pray like the Devil did.

The Devil after having done his job by his book, turned to do some other business of putting some other person astray at some other place. And Shaitan made an Abid a sinner. If the Abid was an Arif he would have said to the Devil when he suggested to him to go to the east side of the town: 'What are you talking? You are a Devil.'

God the Exalted said in the Holy Quran, Aayet 20:14:

And perform the prayer to remember Me.

And God said: Tafakkar Fiddin – put on the thinking cap in the religion.

The gracious sayings - the *Ahadith-e Mubarak* of Hazrat Mohammad Mustufa SAWW:

A person with his manners (*Aekhlaq*) can attain the same rank, which an Abid does with his all night prayer.

A person, who learns one gate of learning, be it only one Hadith, God writes for him *Sawab* – the reward of the virtue of seventy prophets.

Worship is of seventy kinds, the best of which is earning of one's living righteously.

The sayings of Hazrat Ali A.S.:

Aek Ghantay Ka Ghaur-o-Fikr, Tamam Raat Ki Aebadat Say Behtar Haai.

One hour's thinking and deliberation is better than standing all night in prayer.

He, who sought dignity without labour, wasted his life in the quest of impossibility.

Whatever happens from God, do not murmur at it, but try to make things easy and be cheerful.

Do not give up peace as it was followed by thy predecessors, and has been the cause of the accumulation of love and affection, and has caused the good and the prosperity of the people.

15

The Superman in Islam

The city of Strasbourg is at the border of France to the east of Paris. There, for the Centre-in-Strasbourg, an Islamic studies group of 25 Western, non-Muslim and Muslim scholars worked in tandem, contributing and pouring in their findings from their countries to the centre about the sixth Imam of the Aehlebaait, Imam Jafar Sadiq A.S., 702 – 765 AD, 83 – 148 AH. The scholars put their theses in French, which was translated and titled 'The Superman in Islam'.

The Scholars found Imam Jafar Sadiq A.S. – a compound of body and soul of unique learnedness - someone out of this world. His knowledge encompassed all the virtual knowledge defined today by the faculties of physics, chemistry, mathematics, philosophy, logic, astronomy, anthropology, Fiqah (Islamic Law), biology, anatomy, geology, literature, *Irfan* (Gnosis), environmental pollution, and theory of light and beyond. Truly the Imam's knowledge encompassed more knowledge than a list like this enumerated here can enumerate.

All the knowledge reaching to the Imam had come to his subconscious self from God, which was beyond the conscious mind of the ordinary man. The heaven highness of the Imam's knowledge was impossible to be attained by the human. He was of such piety and of such exemplary human qualities that the angles longed to be near to the fringes of the Imam's pieties and his divinities. It was where epistemology failed in inceptions and in its jurisdictions to explain and define what knowledge was and define the veracities of the Imam's knowledge. And at best the human faculty limited in itself to identify the Imam, identified him only as the Superman in Islam.

Imam Jafar Sadiq A.S. founded the Shia Fiqah. He created pupils of such stature at his great university of divine precedence in Medina that excelled in sciences, Fiqah, virtuousness of soul and peeping through the curtain of obscurity into God perceptions. At least forty thousand students and four Sunni Fiqah(s) emerged to elate the Muslims from the Imam's learning centre in Medina. And all the four Sunni Fiqah(s) were strong enough to compete with the Shia Fiqah. So methodical and high level of knowledge imparting was the Imam's compatibility with the absolute Knowledge - the God.

The esoteric power and the zenith of the depth of knowledge of the Imams of the House of the Prophet Mohammad Mustufa SAWW cannot be gauged who were each equal in knowledge and in divine authority, and the scholars could best sum it up, using the phrase of 'Super Man' in the case of Imam Jafar Sadiq A.S. whose life and work they studied within their scopes of the limits of the accessibility to facts by them.

Imam Jafar Sadiq A.S. was 11 years of age in 713 AD, when he said that the sun did not go round the earth - as was the belief at the time given by the hypotheses of Aristotle, Euclid and Ptolemy. He said that the earth goes round the sun and it spins on its axis. The discovery of Copernicus that the earth revolves round the sun came in the 15th century. Likewise, Galileo's observation that the earth spins on its axis came in 1610, about 800 years after the revelation by the Imam.

The Imam talked of the atmospheric pollution, blood circulation in the body and of the minute life cells. The complete knowledge on blood circulation came when William Harvey the English physician submitted his treatise in 1628. The Imam's other scientific contribution was on the theory of light, based on which binoculars and telescopes were made. But most of all, the Imam was the saviour of Shiaism that has a unique system of creating learned Aayetullahs - the PhDs, free of fallacies, who are primes of the religious doctrines on earth.

The Twelve Imams of the House of the Prophet SAWW in authority, divine knowledge and piety were equal to each other and each of them was appointed by God and each of them was *Masoom* or infallible. Imam Jafar Sadiq A.S.'s Great, Grandfather, Imam Husain A.S. is Karim - Ibn Karim, Ibn Karim, Ibn Karim (son of one who wants nothing from one opposite him and only gives). The attribute of Imam Husain A.S. near God is he is Sayyadush - Shuhada – the pinnacle of martyrdom. Imam Jafar Sadiq A.S. says about Imam Husain A.S.:

If God wants someone's wellbeing, He SWT puts love of Husain in his heart.

Other sayings of Imam Jafar Sadiq A.S.:

It is possible that the literature may have no knowledge, but there is no knowledge without literature.

The doubt about idol worshipping is the beginning of the worship of Allah.

Sayings of Imam Husain A.S.:

Fa Inni La Ara Al Maut, Illa Saadatan Wa La Al Hayata Ma Aa Al-Zalimina, Illa Barama (Taghful Aqool, p. 245).

I find death, good fortune, and living with oppressors, dishonour.

The favours should be like the heavy rain which covers the pious and the sinful both.

Beware of things for which you apologise. The true believer should not make mistakes and should not apologise. The hypocrite makes mistakes and apologises every day.

Saying of Hazrat Ali A.S.:

The following six things are the best tests on one's wisdom:

1. To forbear at the time of anger.

2. To be steadfast at the time of danger.

3. To follow moderation at the time of temptation.

4. To be pious under all circumstances.

5. To be on friendly terms with people at large and

6. To abstain from quarrelling with others.

16

The Reformer and the Taliban

A social reformer said to a hard-core Taliban, 'It is understandable that you carry gun and gun down someone who you find against your Shariat laws that you are out to impose on everyone. But what is not understandable is that why you boycott fish and do not eat fish.'

'It is a fine food and not forbidden by the Shariat and so many fish are found in your rivers?'

The Taliban said, 'I do not eat fish because fish is Haram.'

'Fish is not Haram, everybody knows that it is Halal and not Haram,' replied the reformer.

The Taliban said, 'Everybody does not know that fish is Haram and not Halal.'

The reformer said, 'How it can be that fish is Haram, when all the pious and the holy, and all the law giving Prophets of the past ate it and told of it being Halal?'

The Taliban said, 'The Molvi Sahib says it is Haram.'

The Taliban said, 'The Molvi Sahib says, 'The fish is Haram, because it is not put to *Zabah* - to slaughtering under the call of Allah-ho-Akbar.'

The reformer was flabbergasted to hear that revelation from the Taliban and said to him, 'You have caught the Molvi Sahib and put aside the Quran. The

Quran says do not recite Quran by swinging your body, but you do just that what the Molvi Sahib says, and recite by swinging your body.'

The reformer said: 'The logic says you listen to the teacher Meesam-e Tammar, who taught lessons from that whom the Prophet SAWW said, he was 'gate of the city of knowledge' i.e. Hazrat Ali A.S., but you listen to that Ibn Abbas who opposed the gate of the city of knowledge.'

The reformer pointed at the Taliban and said, 'You listen to the Molvi Sahib who gives warped knowledge about religion. He quotes unverified, non-genuine Hadith and non-genuine exegesis of Quran, and you do not exercise rationality and listen to him and cram what he says.'

'And the trouble is you have every year 200,000 Molvis turned out from the Madrasas. You have 17,000 registered and 12,000 unregistered Madrasas in Pakistan, in which there are 3 million Taliban under coaching, who are trained by these Molvis and there are 5 million Molvis around in the country with a yearly budget of Rs 20 billion, pumped in by the affluent and the Arabs to serve these Madrasas.'

The Taliban refuted all that assumption by the reformer and denied any reduction in their zeal for true Islam and raised the musket and the length of its gun barrel at the reformer and said to the reformer:

'Khoochah, Hum Tum Ko Naheen Chhorday Ga, Goli Maray Ga Tum Molvi Sahib Ko Jhoota Bolta Haai.'

Khoochah, I will not spare you, I'll hit you with bullet, you utter to say Molvi Sahib is in the wrong.

Ahadith of the Prophet of God, Hazrat Mohammad Mustufa SAWW:

God severely dislikes quarrelsome and crooked talking person.

A person, who wants to talk to God, should read Quran.

A person who enters into one door of knowledge, even if it is one Hadith, God writes for him *Sawab* (the reward of virtue) of seventy Prophets.

An excellent help to guard against evil is wealth.

Saying of Hazrat Ali AS.:

Every defect can be removed but stupidity, and every disease can be cured but ill temper.

Think over thy existence, when the hair of thy head turns gray. Die faithful and be the winner of the best carpet in the tomb.

Do not tarnish the light of thy old age with sins.

Every wound has a specific medicine, but there is no remedy for ill-manners.

17

The Taliban and the Jew

The birth of the Taliban is related with Jang-o-Jadal – the armed clashes. But they outstrip decency and a fair fight and wade into inhumanness and barbarism. A video shows a Taliban is cutting the neck of a Pakistani Army Soldier with knife and two Taliban press the body of the Shaheed[9] soldier on the ground. Another video shows 14 or 15 civilians standing in a line, and one Taliban shoots in their heads from behind. Their bodies fall. The Taliban then triumphantly makes a speech, warning others of their fates. The Taliban high command, suspected these civilians were hostile.

Napoleon Bonaparte was a conqueror, a sophisticated ruler, a writer and a humanist. He says:

---

[9] Extremism is cultivated by all the Sunni Deo Bandi political parties in Pakistan. The Jamaat-e Islami Chief, Munawar Hasan says, 'the army soldiers killed by the Taliban are not Shaheed, they are Halak - not have died an honourable death for fighting a war with the Americans (both having similar objective against terrorists). Munawar Hasan is an ally of the Taliban and follows the same Shariat as the Taliban. He is working for Taliban, defaming the Pakistan Army and demoralising the nation to defeatism. The Tablighee Jamaat, Jamaat-e Islami and the Masjid Walay have duty to create supporters for the Taliban and work for creating financial resources for them. There are experts of bank robbery, car lifting, extortion and abduction for serving the Taliban. All this debasing of self is to control the army and resist the Twelvers Shias at all cost.

The world suffers a lot, not because of the violence of the bad people, but because of the silence of the good people.

The Taliban kill not because they have a cause and honour to defend but kill because they hate. They kill Shia pilgrims going to and coming back from Ziarat. They make blasts in the Imam Baargah, in the mosques and terrorize the population. The Taliban like Jangrez Khan, Son of Kala Khan from race Khalil Mehmand, plays football with the heads they cut to terrorise. They want to rule Pakistan with their interpreted Islamic Sharia and want it as superior law in the countries of Afghanistan and Pakistan.

Volumes of evidences exist that the country of Pakistan is being pushed in the lap of the Taliban. The PMLN, PTI, Jamaat-e Islami, Jamiatay Ulema-ay Pakistan Samiul Haque, Jamiat Ulema-e Islam Fazlul Haque Group in Pakistan are with the Taliban. This is ominous and a sign of disaster. The fear hangs on the heads of the Shia intellectuals and the Shia professionals that their lives will be taken any time soon. The Taliban policy is to clear Pakistan of the Shias. Pakistan is now a dictatorial regime, not ruled by the Islamic constitution written by the God fearing of the nation of the past but ruled by the fanatic with their finger on the trigger of the gun.

The government of the PMLN started their rule in May 2013. They are mainly interested in prolonging their rule. They would rather side with the gun slinging Taliban to gain period to rule, than see social justice and ethics come to prevail. Consequently terror is on the rise and the decadence of ethics taking root.

The Taliban want everyone to become pure Muslim under their Sharia. They want everyone to have long beard and wear baggy Shalwar, which stays above the ankles and prominently shows the left and the right ankles. They want the *Twelvers Ulema* - the Shia scholars who are so high in purity of faith and so strong a barrier against injustice and division in religion that they even reject Sufism and *Kashf* – the intuitive knowledge (which might be an intentional or casual deviation from the truism of Islam), eliminated as Ulema of Islam.

These Ulema are the *Asas* – the roots of Islam, who follow *Irfan* (Gnosticism) and are *Usuli*[10] - the rationalists. The Taliban are against the Shia Ulema, because with them around the Taliban will never succeed with their *Khwariji* – the external to Islam tendencies.

The nearest definition quantifying the Taliban is; they are unratified Muslims. They are *Takfiri* or infidels, who do not consider Hadith and Quran and *Ijtehad* (research) as the sources of law to be ruled by, but have their own carved Sharia they created to dominate Islam. They consider attack on Church permissible by Shariat. They want to declare all the *Sahaba* or companions of the Prophet SAWW *Masoom* or infallible, and want them to look monumental beings, greater than the God purified Mutahhar of the House

---

[10] Our salutes to the Aayetullah(s) and the Ulemas of the school of the Twelve Imams for keeping the pattern and the style of the life of the Twelve Imams alive and going, and for Hujjat – the proof of God to show its bright face to the world through their countenances.

of the Prophet SAWW. They say Prophet SAWW is dead and disregard Quran, which says otherwise.

The Taliban want religious education taught in schools, but only that what will serve promote to bring their rule. And in all cases want girls over ten years not to go to school. They want everyone to go to the mosque five times a day for prayers and if anyone found outside, they will send him to the mosque to pray. And if he said he had said his prayer already, the Taliban will send him to pray again in the mosque. They only tell the Shia peoples not to go to the mosque and tell them that they can say their prayers in their houses. The Shia rationale on this erraticism – erosion of faith replied to the Taliban by quoting Aayet 10:86 of the Holy Quran:

And by Thy mercy save us from the transgression of the Kafir race (the deniers practicing oppression).

The Talban for such prototype replies hated the Shias and in their Khiffat – slight and disgrace, despite the Shias' learning and knowledge called them Kafirs. They hated the Hindus[11] for their humility and resilience, and the Buddhists for their monk habits and their beliefs of *Kamma*, and their strength of *Wasila* - the intercessor approach – inhibiting them follow other religions. And they hated the Sunni Muslims if they were against their neo-religion they preached in Islam, and if the mild Sunnis were accommodating to the

---

[11] There are some Hindus, some Patel families in Brent and Kensal Rise in London who mourn Imam Husain A.S. for ten days. The irony is, no Taliban or a far left Sunni Muslim will mourn Imam Husain A.S. for ten days.

Shias. According to them the Sunnis should have no sympathy for the Shias in their hearts. They hated everyone other than their Taliban varieties and considered others *Mushrakoon* - the polytheists.

Ansar Ali is an elderly Shia from village Asterzaee in the mountains near Kohat. Asterzaee is purely a Shia village and Ansar Ali says they cannot go out of the house. The Taliban are all over. Little boys inform the Taliban by their mobile phone and they come to shoot to kill. Ansar Ali says our lookouts on the hills in their posts work day and night and guard and protect the village and that's how we live. He says the conditions have deteriorated since Benazir is gone.

All this unhappy state in the Muslim world has come about, since it is devoid of a supreme coordinating institution like of the 'Wilayat-e Faqih', headed by a Wali al-Faqih, such as Seyed Ali Hoseini Khamenei in Iran or any such body which will solve differences and remove friction and clashes between the factions in Islam.

The Taliban are neither politicians, nor a learned class, nor an average citizen of approximate moderate professional status who will work to support a society. They are plain ignorant and paupers of knowledge, but consider themselves *Quran Daan* – knowledge holders of Quran, and *Muminoon* – the believers, and *Salihoon* – the virtuous, and consider all other dirt and look at them scornfully.

The Ameer of the outlawed Tahreek-e Taliban Pakistan, Hakeem Ullah Mehsud was responsible for killing 50,000 innocent Pakistanis. He was a wanted man, who was finally killed on November 1, 2013 by a Pakistani-American drone armed with missile, about which the ex-president of Pakistan, General Pervez Musharraf explains: 'There was a pact between America and Pakistan that the Americans will locate the terrorists by using satellite and aerial vehicles, and share the information with the Pakistan Army, who will take ground action against these miscreants.'

But the information to the army was leaked out to the Taliban by the Taliban sympathisers. This led the Americans to do independent operations. The Pakistan government was not entirely apathetic to these judicious operations of the Americans, only the killing of Hakeem Ullah Mehsud displeased the new Talibanized government of the PMLN, who raised all kinds of hue and cry. Hakeem Ullah Mehsud had said to a journalist before he was drone attacked and killed:

Musalmanoan ki Humnay Tareef Ki Haai Ki Musalman Kaun Ho Sakta Haai, Woh Jo Taghoot say Barayat Ka Aelan Kartay Haain.

I have defined a Muslim that who can be a Muslim, those who declare they oppose Taghoot or the devil.

This statement shows as if he is the authority to define a Muslim. With such arrogance and his killing the innocent citizens, he was called martyr by Ameer Jamaat Islami, Mr Munawar Hasan. Hakeem Ullah Mehsud is an object of veneration and pilgrimage to him, but the *Adl* – the justice of God says he is not a martyr. In any case this distinction of a martyr has little meaning for them as their whole Fiqah is based on boycotting visits to the graves.

The Prophet SAWW has said:

Al Muslimo Mun Salama Al Muslemoon Mun Yadhi Wa Lesaneh.

Muslim is that from whose hand and tongue the Muslim people remain safe.

By this Hadith, Hakeem Ullah Mehsud does not qualify to be called a Muslim, let alone he accorded the status of a martyr. The scholars called such people and groups, *Khwarij* – those who went out of the orbit of Islam. And it was bias and self-deception to call him a martyr by the Jamaat-e Islami Chief, Munawar Hasan. They may venerate and idolize him, but cannot give him the status of a martyr. The Aayet 4:65 says:

(O Messenger) on oath of your God, these people will not be true Momin[12], until they make you commander for the judgement of what is in dispute between them; not only that but what judgement you give, if they do not feel miserly, but happily own it.

The Prophet's judgement and his most powerful directive to his nation of believers are in the Hadith:

A man will die the death of Jahilia – of ignorance, if he did not recognise the Imam of his time.

---

[12] The difference between the Momin and the Muslim is that the Momin is submissive to the Wilayet of Hazrat Ali A.S., but the hypocrites are generally unconcerned with it or deny of it.

And the Imam of the time is the twelfth descendant Imam, Imam Mehdi A.S. in the line of the Imamat of Hazrat Ali A.S.

Another Hadith of the Prophet SAWW which describes and codifies the virtues of the Imams from the Aehlebaait and which is the most effective tool of reform and of the checks and balance in Islam is:

'Of the Twelve Imams, the first is Mohammad, the middle is Mohammad, the last is Mohammad and all are Mohammad.'

So the Imam is to be found in the House of the Prophet SAWW. But Hakeem Ullah Mehsud and his supporters search their Imams in the houses other than that of the Prophet SAWW and kill *Taqleedi* (conformist) *Imami* Muslims or the Shias, which speaks of their non-adherence to these Ahadith and their silent revolt against Islam.

After Hakeem Ullah Mehsud's death, his two wives are in *Iddat* – probationary period for the widows, but his two wives, Mohtarma Begum Orilia and Mohtarma Ansaran Begum - Mari Wali, both of who were working as his *Daashta* or concubines and were not in Nikah, are receiving condolences for their husband's death, for which a head money of 5 carore (50 million) rupees was placed by the previous government of Pakistan.

The Americans are now entitled to this money who received none of it. Instead the government of PMLN, PTI, and the political parties, Jamaat Islami and JUI, and all the Talibanized parties are accusing the Americans for killing Mehsud and are mourning his death.

Maulana Samiul Haque, Head of the JUI (S) says he is father of the Taliban. His manifesto is all high offices of the state should be held by the Sunni Muslim men. He says whatever is the demand of the Taliban is his demand. The Talibanized PMLN interior minister, Nisar Ali Khan paid Mehsud tribute by calling his death, 'death of the peace efforts'. He said, 'Every aspect of Pakistan's cooperation with Washington will be revised following Mehsud's killing.' This leaves no misgivings that Pakistan is way gone Taliban.

Hakeem Ullah Mehsud was the TTP chief with an avowed policy to target and kill anyone they considered anti-Taliban. He was killed by the 317th drone attack unleashed against the terrorist on 1 November 2013. The statistics say 2160 terrorists were killed by 317 drone attacks since it started in 2008, but it also killed 67 innocent Pakistanis, which is grieved by the Pakistan nation.

History will remember the farcicality of the Ameer Jamaat Islami, Munawar Hasan. Besides calling Hakeem Ullah Mehsud a martyr, he called Pakistan Army Soldiers who fought alongside the Americans against the Taliban, *Halak* – not Shaheed. Earlier, on 15 September 2013, the Taliban martyred Major General Sana Ullah Niazi and Lt. Col. Tauseef by bomb blast and then boasted on the YouTube: they sent them to hell. Such far gone extremism and debauching is due to the political support to the Taliban by the Pakistan Deo Bandi political parties – the PMLN, PTI, JI, and JUI factions, who all are riding in one boat.

It is sad, how moralistic stand and Quranic edicts to punish murderers can be sacrificed at the altar of the grab for power through the obduracy of the unconstitutional negotiations by the PMLN's government with the Taliban. The army could take no action to punish the murderers of their martyrs – the Shuhada, because of the government's subjective tendency towards the Taliban and the Jamaat-e Islami party's negativity towards the army. This allowed the Taliban to warm up to bully and warn the Media:

'If their views were not reported favourably, unspecified action will be taken against them.'

And this made the Rooh of the Shuhuda restless as it was not answered positively by their fellow military men, due to army inhibited by the government from taking military action against the Taliban.

Nadaan Ki Dosti Ghatay Ki Kheti Haai

Friendship of a naive friend is harvesting of disadvantages the army was better off keeping the government at bay.

The army's collective knowledge is more than of a dictatorial individual, especially an unprincipled prime minister, diversionary in practice (see p. 16). And the religion of the army[13] is service to the nation. The army has right to take corrective action in the interest of country and its honour. If there is such a prime minister in the saddle, whose hidden is different than

---

[13] I was in the 11th JSPCTS at Quetta in 1953, and made Prefect of the Tochi House for my term of the assignment, and 'had the taste of the fidelity of the army. What a great institution it is. There is every evidence and Godly proof that God loves them, because they love each other. Pray it marches on with its traditions.

apparent, for the sake of sanity, reason and service to nation, he should be removed. Our much maligned General Ziaul Haque was right when he said, 'Constitution is a piece of paper'. It is only a ruling to be followed if honour is not reduced through its binds.

For all the chicken fixings JI's Munawar Hasan did for Mehsud, the Facebook was sardonic to him and advised friends to read poet Iqbal's proverb, *'Jafar Uz Bengal Aur Sadiq Uz Dakan'*, in these words:

Munawar Uz Dilli Aur Maudoodi Uz Dakan
Nang-e Millat, Nang-e Deen, Nang-e Watan.

Munawar from Delhi and Maudoodi from Deccan,
Disgrace of the nation, disgrace of the religion, (and) disgrace of the country.

The language of the sane wants the above *Misra* - the verse replace the old, since the *Behr* or the weightage and the sound of the new line are better matched by the poetic synthesis and the new characters in the verse are beating the old characters in betrayal.

The origin of the Taliban was in the creation of civilian cum military fighters. And they were named 'Mujahedeen' - religious fighters with a political imbibe to fight against the Russians. The Russians had entered in Afghanistan in 1979 and the Mujahedeen were raised to kill and destabilise the Russians. They were picked from the Pashtoon clans by the Afghan warlords and the Mullas picked them from the Madrasas and a Major General of the Pakistan Army, trained them with the objective to gain strategic depth in the Afghan land. The Americans financed the scheme to avenge the humiliation they had suffered in Vietnam at the hands of the Russians. And greed and avenge were responsible for the creation of the Taliban.

The Mujahedeen became Taliban in 1993 after the soviets left Afghanistan in 1990. Soon their cult of vengeance against the Shias of the Northern Alliance became their faith and policy. It became a strong tree of hatred against all the Shias. The Taliban became leaders and champions of the Sunni faiths[14]. And since all power comes from the barrel of gun, they took to arm them to the teeth with sophisticated guns and make blasts and create a tailored Shariat. The money came from loot, drug and donations - foreign and indigenous.

But just as they tailored the Shariat wrong, their idiocy and their poor linguistic knowledge and poor etymology inflected them select their name wrong. The word 'Taliban'meant, 'people who want' - this word was not right vis-à-vis the intended meaning of 'the students'. Only its *Istelahi* - the intentional meaning introduced by the Madrasas was 'religious student'. But it was not a *Lughvi* or dictionary meaning. The word chosen should have been *Tullab* —

---

[14] Every day the Sunni faith is weakening because its representations are being faked by the extremists whose factions are given birth with the diversity in the political scenario of countries backing them. The collective Sunnism may be suffering, but still great is the Sunni Aalim with his shining face, who's Wazoo – the ablution is Wahdaniat or Oneness of God and reflection on his face, from the brilliance of the countenance of the Prophet SAWW.

which is plural of *Talib* – the student, which they would like to be taken as, and understood as. So the very basis of their name and move is crooked and they are a contemptible species and they kill and do bloodshed.

It is in the blood of the Taliban not to remain peaceful. They bomb shrines of Shia *Akabereen* – the revered pious, and bomb schools. They blew up the statues of Gautam Buddha in Bamiyan in 2001 in Afghanistan and the Buddha statues in Pakistan in Mangalore in 2007. They have created law and order problem in Pakistan and have ruined its peace and blocked its scientific and cultural progress.

They have taken up violence and killing for God, though it is not a cause of God. The new Ameer of the outlawed Tahreek-e Taliban Pakistan, Mulla Fazlullah has head money on him, and yet he was appointed Ameer by the Taliban factions five days after their Ameer Mehsud was drone attacked on 1 November 2013. Mulla Fazlullah says boisterously:

Sub Say Pahlay Pakistan say Shioan Ka khatima Kareingay. Pakstani Fauj Mein Aksariat Shia Ki Haai.

Before anything else (I'll) finish the Shias first from Pakistan. The Pakistani army has majority of the Shias.

And regardless of this dissention and the proclamation of an intended crime, the government of the PMLN is going to negotiate with them and this so when they do not even accept the constitution of the country. They call the parliament un-Islamic and illegitimate. The Taliban extremists have so ruined the image of

Pakistan in the world that the innocent Laila Agarwal from Sardarshahar India, says in the Facebook chat:

'Kyu ki Pakistan ka naam aesa hai na, isliye sab unko pasand nahi karte hai. Kissi bhi country me puchh lo aap.'

'Because the name of Pakistan is such - truly so, everyone is not liking them. You ask in any country.'

The Taliban trained their suicide bombers in the Swat Valley. The training school showed pictures of a simulated Jannat painted on the walls. They said to the suicide bombers, it is where you will go after suicide bombing. They have killed 65,000 citizens of Pakistan; still Pakistan is their safe haven, because more than half of the Pakistani nation is Taliban minded.

The journalists, bureaucrats, judiciary, politicians, Mullas, all are semi Taliban in Punjab, which forms 60% of the population of the country. If the Shia Momeneen were not living in the country, the country with the burden of its injustices, apoplectic ways and its burden of the pig-headed obduracy will collapse.

The outspoken defendant of the Taliban, Fareed Paracha of the Jamaat-e Islami party, in a TV talk show will never call Taliban – *Zalim*, i.e. tyrant, aggressor and murderer. Even when cornered in the argument. He will deceive and parry question and defend the Taliban (ref: 'News Beat' of 14 December 2013).

In this programme Allama Tahir Ashrafi is another irritant. He will not abandon his indirect support for the Lashkar-e Jhangvi, who kill Shias and openly claim so. The Taliban wanted to stop the Juloos of the

Chehlam in Rawalpindi to pass through its traditional route on 24 December 2013. They also wanted Azadari confined to the boundary walls of the Imam Baargahs. But the Chehlam Juloos on 24 December 2013 passed through its old route. It was led by the Ulema and thousands of *Mominas* (the female pious Muslims), who came out with their children in the juloos.

It was the longest Juloos ever; several kilometres long and all the terrorist groups who had vowed not to allow the Juloos pass through its old route were beating their chests in grief and blaming the Sunnat Wal Jamaat Ulema for not siding with them. The Facebook posts are full of the Taliban laments. It is a defeat of terrorism and the beginning of the good bye to the Taliban. This is a present to the nations from Imam Husain A.S.

Then the fiery speech of the young politician and Chairman Bilawal Bhutto on 27 December slapped the Taliban and dampened their daredevilry. The speech defined the friends of Taliban - *Ghaddar* i.e. traitors. He gave the catchphrase - *Jo Talban kay Yar Haain Mulk Kay Ghaddar Haain*, and named Imran Khan, 'Buzdil Khan' for appeasing the Taliban (apparently fearing them). Bilawal Bhutto gave the Taliban one choice; to throw down their weapon and accept Islam and the constitution of Pakistan or face annihilation. This speech and the longest procession in Rawalpindi was a deathblow to the Taliban terrorism.

The Al Qaeda's Aiman Al Zawahiri, in the days of their rising stars, said, 'We need a region in Pakistan where we can form our government'. The Tehreek-e Taliban Pakistan demanded a similar state as Al Zawahiri did.

They demanded that the Pak Army clear off from Waziristan, also the constitution of Pakistan be amended, for a constitutional basis for their takeover of the entire country.

They have support of the Arab Wahabi states and are waiting for the end of the year 2014, when the American and other NATO forces will leave Afghanistan. Then the combined Afghanistan and Pakistan Taliban forces will conquer these countries for the glory of Wahabism and the sustainability of the Arab kingdoms.

The political parties, PMLN, PTI, JI, JUI in Pakistan are backing the Taliban and their dividend is that in the general election in May 2013 in Pakistan, the Tehreek-e Taliban Pakistan, issued threats to all the liberal, neutral and anti-Taliban parties that their meetings will be bombed. The Punjab Taliban kidnapped Ali Haider, son of the PPP ex-Prime Minister Yusuf Raza Gilani to stop their election campaign. They threatened the PPP and their ally ANP voters not to go to vote and these parties shrank.

The Taliban permitted only those political parties to campaign in the general election which saw eye to eye about their politico-religious agenda for the country. They campaigned without fear of bullets and suicide bombing and the PMLN won in the election in 2013 albeit also their rigging of the election and formed the government in Pakistan. But they are challenged against vote rigging and ballot paper swapping in 32 seats and Faisal Raza Abedi says only 56 seats are right, rest have been won through rigging, all over the country.

The PMLN after winning the seats for the parliament, to thank the Taliban, called an All Parties Conference (APC) on 9 September, 2013. Not one Shia political party was invited by the PMLN to appease the Taliban. And the terrorists were called 'stakeholders'. And their case to ban the drone attack was promised to be taken to the UNO General Assembly.

The Taliban have mushroomed into sixty-two groups and all are example of terror and extortion. The Taliban extortionists demanded four carore (forty million) rupees from a Shia on phone. The Shia used to hold Majlis-e Husain on the 15th of Moharram each year on a large scale in Karachi. After Majlis food was served as Tabarruk. The Taliban said you have money and give us from that. The Shia ignored their demand, so next he received an envelope with two bullets in it and a note. The note said, 'Which dead body you want first, your young son's or your daughter's?' The Shia bought air tickets for his family of four, and left his job and the house and left Pakistan the next night on asylum to England.

The Taliban are in each street of Pakistan, they daily spill innocent blood there. They recruit ignorant countrymen as Taliban sacrificial devotee and break open gate when they have become Taliban criminals and take them away from the jails, and export them in squads from Pakistan to places like Syria. And daily shoot and kill Shia Intellectuals: professors, doctors, lawyers, Ulemas and thinkers.

They tore up the pages of the internal-medicine books in the bookshops in Kabul, since these carried illustrative nude sketches of women and men in its pages. They considered it vulgarism! No woman in their regime in Afghanistan was allowed out of the house unless she was all covered in Burqa and was with an escort. The women were repressed, flogged and stoned and were frightened prisoners in their house during the Taliban rule in Afghanistan.

Bertrand Russell in his book Power, published in 1938, p. 224 of the Routledge Classics 2004 says: (Quoted by Philosopher Derek Foster of Pinner Philosophy Group in his talk 'Russell on Power', September 2013):

'In passing by the side of mount Thai, Confucius came on a woman who was weeping bitterly by a grave. The Master pressed forward and drove quickly to her, then he sent Tze-Lu to question her. "You're wailing", said he, "is that of one who has suffered sorrow on sorrow?" She replied, "That is so. Once my husband's father was killed here by a tiger, my husband was also killed, and now my son has died in the same way."

The Master said, "Why do you not leave this place?" The answer was "There is no oppressive government here." The Master then said, "Remember this my children: oppressive government is more terrible than tigers." And this explains the state Pakistan is in, and the reason why the Shia family left Pakistan on asylum to England.

The Taliban ruled Afghanistan from 1996 – 2001. In this period, a brave Jew lived in Kabul. He was living alone for a long time and strictly followed Judaism. A Taliban for a long time was breathing down his neck, asking him to become a Muslim. The Jew bravely resisted the conversion effort by the Taliban and also did not leave Kabul. But his life had become miserable. The Taliban was nagging him all the time to convert to Islam. So one day the Jew gave up and said to the Taliban, 'All right I become a Muslim, tell me the Kalima'

The Taliban said to the Jew, 'you miserable Jew, you don't know the Kalima? You menace! You think I know that thing? Khana Kharab (horrid misery) if I knew wouldn't I tell you?'

The Jew said, 'All you non-Jews are donkeys and you bonkers, pestering me to be Muslim, when you don't know what makes one a Muslim!'

The Prophet SAWW one day so addressed his Sahaba:

'Like of the past *Ummats* (the nations) you too are struck with a disease, and that is jealousy. This illness does not eat up material wealth but eats up *Deen* – the religion. The way to get rid of it is that man withholds himself and keeps his tongue tied and does not taunt and reproach his Momin brother.'

Again the Prophet Hazrat Mohammad Mustufa SAWW said, (Ref. Al-Badaya Wal Nehaya 231- 8):

'*Amr* (the ordinance) of my Ummat will remain enforce with justice, till the first person who will destroy it, will be from Bani Umayya, who will be called Yazid.'

Sayings of Hazrat Ali A.S.:

Do not listen to the man, whose speech annoys thee, and never mind the abusive words used in thy absence by a back-biter, as if they were not uttered at all.

There will come a time when only the letters of the Quran and merely the name of Islam will remain. The mosques though exceedingly beautiful and highly magnificent will be entirely devoid of light and learning.

Obligation subdues hearts, and charity hides faults.

18

The Black Burqa and the Hijab

Of the two friends – the recently married and the long married, the recently married was sitting head down, sad and brooding. The long married came to him and said, 'What is the matter with you? These are the best days of life and you are down and grieved.'

The recently married said, 'Brother, it was a very bad day for me.'

The long married said, 'Sad to know that! Tell me what happened.'

The recently married said, 'My wife and I went to a *Mehfil* (a gathering). There I walked to my wife, she was standing in a group with others; all were wearing Burqa. I put my arm on the shoulders of my wife, but it was not my wife, instead it was a brute lady. She turned and gave me a whacking big slap on my face. It was like a stone hitting the cheek and my cheek is still burning with the heat of the slap.'

'Besides that earlier in the day I was given the sack by the owner of the company. He suspected me to be anti-Taliban, a Shia or something - an Ahmadia or a Lama, as I did not smile and showed no glee when he mentioned the name of the Taliban. And the worst of all this is, when I met my wife just before you came to see me, she showed me the doctor's report which said she has bone disease, rickets; as she is suffering from the deficiency of vitamin D.'

The long married was very sorry to hear all that mishap happening to his recently married friend, and asked him, 'Why your wife is suffering from the deficiency of vitamin D?'

The recently married replied, 'Because she wears thick black Burqa which shuts off sunlight reaching to her bones.'

The long married said, 'Then why your wife not gives up covering herself in thick black Burqa?'

The recently married replied, 'She cannot give up Burqa. The senior Taliban roam in our place with sticks in their hands, forcing Burqa on the women.'

The long married said, 'My wife is from Khorasan near Turkmenistan and all these long years has only covered her head, arms, legs and bosom, and not gone beyond that what is said in the Aayet 33:59 in Quran and she never had any problem with sunlight not touching her bones. She has no disease like your wife has, of rickets.'

'Though I must admit, I am worried about my two little girls who go to school in black Abaya and Hijab. The teacher in the Madrasa demands them to come there all covered, wearing Abaya and Hijab. And I fear they will turn to thick black Burqa soon and will equally suffer with rickets as your wife does.'

The recently married said, 'Yes we need a change of habit and taking to unassuming, simple, compatible culture, unobtrusive to others and staying within the bounds of our religious dictates. We need rules introduced like of the President Nicolas Sarkozy in his country France. He has banned Burqa in his country. He says, it deprives women of their identity and makes them alienated, regimental, snobbish and different from others.'

The recently married at his mention of Sarkozy showed a glee on his face and said with musing: 'And do you know, Sarkozy cannot be challenged that he is violating the edicts of Quran. The spirit of Purdah in Aayet 33:59 is to identify your nobility and protect your *Iffat* – the chastity and not to bring alienation for you from other classes.'

The recently married further added to the dialectical logic and said, 'If such a rule was here, I would not have received slap from the woman in Burqa. If the woman was in Chador or Pashmina, with or without *Maqna* and not wearing a thick black Burqa with a black shield covering her face, as also my wife wears, I would have recognised her after seeing her face that she was not my wife and would not have put my hand on her shoulders.'

The long married replied, 'Women are species driven by self-protectionism that's why she slapped you! They are illogical and work against the dictates of natural justice and not by conscious dictated requirements. They are carrying Purdah beyond that desired. The Saudi women even go for *Tawaf* – the circumambulation of Khana-ay Kaaba in Burqa, hiding their face, which is against the Tawaf edicts.'

The recently married said, 'In spite of these shortcomings of our women and their culture of the abeyance of the display of capabilities and their denounces of the incumbent upon them, let's yield; our chivalry demands that we treat them as equals, as they are treated in the country of President Nicolas Sarkozy, where they show their responsibility to meet all social requirements of the modern day society in learning, debate and judiciousness, beside showing their legitimate egotism. So why our women will not show all these traits, together with their *Mashraqiat* – the Eastern quality, which no one wants them sweep under the carpet, but it cannot be taken as remedy to wipe out sociability - this is impropriety.'

The recently married added, 'Sad, in all this display of woman-ness, our women show less judicious independence in matters related with the social needs of an elated society which is making our culture's humility look small to the host countries and hurtful to their ego. They show more in the display of egotism to satiate their womanhood than contributing to beautifying the environment. They are making it a lopsided stressful profession of a specialist *Burqedari* – the fashion of observance of the rig of Burqa, and not showing they possess a brainy head.'

The long married said, 'True, what you say brother! Also I wonder, why not our women for the sake of human dignity take a step forward and go to the basics in Purdah and take to the Chadar and Maqna of Bibi Zainab SUA and Bibi Fatimah Zehra SUA and emancipate themselves to give vogue to Chador and Maqna,[15] rather than wear a thick black Burqa.'

---

[15] Maqna is a thin cloth. It was worn by Arab women to cover their hair. It was used on the Naushah - the bridegroom in India to

The long married seconded the recently married and further said; 'I second you whole heartedly there. There is only one incidence in the history of Burqa when the thick black Burqa showed its efficacy. It only once in its unholy creation proved congenial; when it helped law and our good General Pervez Musharraf.

The long married said to the recently married, you remember when Molvi Abdul Aziz tried to escape from justice, hiding behind the wall of a thick black Burqa, trying to dodge the nation to help rascality. Well! He was spotted and caught by men on alert because of the smug of the Burqa!'

The recently married said, 'Yes Brother! Still, in spite of that silent service of the Burqa, Chadar is the best as you say, with or without Maqna.' And the recently married became pensive and emotional and showed successive emotions and said: 'O Bibi Zainab! Thou shouldst be living at this hour...'

Then he quoted Mir Anis' narration of the Chador of Bibi Zainab SUA in Karbala:

Jo Na Lay Jana Thha Woh Bhi Sub Sitam Gar Lay Ga-ay
Sheh Ka Malboos-e Kohan Zainab Ki Chadar Lay Ga-ay

What the tyrants had not to take away, they took away Shah's old attire and Zainab's Chador, they took away.

---

cover his face as it drops down on the face from over the Safa or turban, which was wound on his head. The elegance and reverence increases with Maqna.

Bibi Zainab SUA was an orator and one most scholarly member of the House of the Prophet SAWW. She was idolised for her learnedness and virtues of leadership. She was an Aalima – a learned. She was granddaughter of Prophet Mohammad Mustufa SAWW, daughter of Bibi Fatimah and Imam Ali A.S and sister of Imam Husain A.S. She established her distinctiveness and credentials in Islam for her power of oratory and leadership. Bibi Zainab is synonymous with her Chadar which was snatched from her head in Karbala by the tyrants of the Yazid's army after they killed her Imam Brother, Imam Husain A.S. along with her nears and dears.

The massacre in Karbala and the snatching of the Chadar was because the Muslims were driven by avarice, and reversion to barbarism and they gave up fine lessons they were given through the Book and the teachings by the Prophet SAWW.

Aayet 33:53 says:

O ye who believe! Enter not the dwellings of the Prophet until you are called....

No following the dictated right enabled the burials of two Caliphs in the house of the Prophet SAWW. They were buried in the house of the Prophet SAWW with no legitimate permission from the heirs of the Prophet SAWW and then the burial of the legitimate heir and grandson Imam Hasan A.S. was denied entrance there and this ignominy led to the future religious disharmonies in Islam.

Sayings of the Prophet of God, Hazrat Mohammad Mustufa SAWW:

The favours that you do to others keep it from mentioning and mention publicly the favour done to you by others.

It is obligatory on a Muslim that when he goes on journey, he tells his brothers (friends in the community) and it is obligatory on others that when that person returns from the journey they go to meet him.

If a person goes to a house of a Momin to meet him then the Provider of the sustenance tells (that person), you came to meet Me. You are My guest and your hosting is obligatory on Me and because you love this Momin I make you claimant of the paradise.

Sayings of Hazrat Ali A.S.:

The greatest difference between *Soorat* and *Seerat* – the face and character is; the face deceives but the character identifies.

Khuda Jameel Haai Woh Jamal Ko Dost Rakhta Haai Aur Apni Aenayat Ka Asar Apnay Bandoan Per Dekhna Chaheta Haai.

God is beautiful. He keeps friends with elegant and wants to see the effect of His bounties on his servants.

Distance yourself from riots and civil disturbance like an adolescent camel which has a back not strong enough for riding, nor has udders for milking.

He who fears God, fears none.

I would not talk of women, as they are faithless. Their words are as uncertain as a gust of wind. They break your hearts and do not mend them, and their hearts are devoid of sincerity.

Woman is evil, all in all, and the worst of it is that one cannot do without her.

Do not consult women, as their opinion and judgement turns you towards weakness and frailty.

19

Khyali Pulau – Building Castles in the Air

King Arthur consoles Sir Bedivere with his final words:

'...I am going a long way With these thou seest – if indeed I go-(For all my mind is clouded with a doubt) To the Island-valley of Avilion; Where falls not hail, or rain, or any snow, Nor ever wind blows loudly; but it lies Deep-meadow'd, happy, fair with orchard-lawns And bowery hollows crown'd with summer sea, Where I will heal me of my grievous wound.' (Lines 256-264 from the Idylls - Tennyson)

Poet Alfred Lord Tennyson uses the metaphor of the valley of Avilion for the paradise and shows complete faith in its existence and its chain of blissful places and the hierarchy of the paradise in the heavens. And he in fact declares he was from one of the believers in the unseen and an establisher of worship. But at the same time, Poet Alfred Tennyson in his life was moody and morose and an excessive drinker, but poet Laureate par excellence.

The poet says (Lines 247 – 56, from the Idylls):

'... More things are wrought by prayer than this world dreams of...'

About freedom of action and destiny the poet says: 'Though men may imagine they have free will, they are ultimately answerable to the Divine Will of God...'

Alfred Tennyson's first son Hallam Tennyson says, 'His father explained to him that 'the Pilot was that Divine and Unseen who is always guiding us.''

So the poet believed in God and had a faith compatible with reality and in harmony with the advocating of Islam and had no dreams but belief in realities.

But our Sheikh Chilli of the Indian legend, daydreams of the fantasies and makes idle schemes. And since no two dreams can be the same unless true, our Sheikh Chilli each day sees a new dream and plans a new scheme. He cooks *Khyali Pulau* — builds imaginative schemes and lives on vain hopes. And dives in dreams to dress impracticalities into imaginative practicalities to get rich, and go a long way in the life.

The country folks tell there was a Mr Shaikh Chilli in the not too far-gone distant days. He was always playing prank and doing funny things and daydreaming. One day he found a hen which was walking as a lone bird. It was wandering and lost. Mr Shaikh Chilli pounced at her and caught her and brought her home and set her to lay eggs.

The hen started laying one egg every day. Mr Sheikh Chilli started building his castle in the air and said when the hen has laid one dozen eggs, he will take them to the market and sell and buy a *Chooza* — a young chick, which soon will grow and become a hen and she will also lay one egg each day.

This way, Mr Sheikh Chilli said, there will be two eggs every day and when there will be twenty-four eggs, he will take them to the market and sell them and buy two young chicks, and they will grow and become hens. So there will be four hens, and he will soon have many hens and sell their eggs and buy a buffalo. The buffalo will give bucketful milk which he will sell and buy two bullocks, and use the bullocks to till the barren land of the Kikar trees that no one wants and is no one's property.

Mr Sheikh Chilli said, he will sow in the barren land and grow crop and sell grain. He will load sacks full of grains on the mules from his grain-barn, which he will fill with crops and drive the mules to the market and he will at once become a merchant, a farmer and sweetly loved and as respected as a magistrate and as rich as the Mahajan and as wise as Akbar-e Azam's Nau Ratan. And the village chief will come on foot personally walking, all friendly and say, 'Hello' Mr Sheikh Chilli!

Mr Sheikh Chilli made all such bright plans for his future, using his *Khyali Pulau* – imaginative schemes. Then on the day, when the eggs he counted were twelve, he put them in a basket and put the basket on his head and rushed for the market, all the way thinking of the buffalo, bullocks and the crops.

On the way, there was a field he had to cross. Suddenly a bull came out of nowhere; it charged, rushing at him and knocked him down to the ground. The basket came crashing down to the ground and all the eggs were broken.

Mr Sheikh Chilli lost all the eggs and with that the dream to get rich, the scheme he planned went to the winds. He picked up himself and began to curse the crazy bull and the dark forces on the earth – the jealousy, revenge, indolence, apathy and all those baddies and said, these deprived him to get rich and be famous. Mr Sheikh Chilli started back for home spitting curses at the bull, when he reached home he went to look if the hen had laid any eggs in the meantime, but found the hen was not in its spot, the hen had run away. Mr Sheikh Chilli spat more curses at the bull.

He blamed the bull for the disaster and when he had cooled his mind, he started a fresh daydream. He said, 'The village Hakeem collects grass and pods from the forest, dries these up and gives them to the patients and has got rich that way. So I should do the Hakeem's work and get rich that way.' And he set out to collect grass and pods and look for the patients. Soon he found plenty of grass and a patient and gave him his grass and pods which infected him with diarrhoea. The patient nearly died, and barely survived.

For the euphoria to get rich with silly schemes and using wrangling and for the pranks and mischief, Mr Sheikh Chilli became very famous among the folks. His name for his mischievous schemes and some miseries he brought to others became the household story with the peoples of his time. His name travelled through the times and carried through it his fame all through the subcontinent of India. But the people cautioned each other not to become a Sheikh Chilli, who for fun was everyone's pony to ride on, and his name used to express ridiculous notions, but his ways were deterred not to be practiced.

Sayings of Prophet Hazrat Mohammad Mustufa SAWW:

Mun Arafa Nafsahoo Faqad Arafa Rabbah.

The person, who discovered his self, discovered his Sustainer (God).

On the day of judgement, the worst man near God is that from whose fear of evil, men have been doing his respect.

The intention of the Momin is better than his deed and the intention of the Kafir (the denier of God) is worse than his deed.

Sayings of Hazrat Ali A.S.:

He, who follows moderation; wealth accompanies him, and his loss and poverty are remedied thereby.

None, but intelligent and painstaking can attain lofty ideals.

Surely, the wealth and the offspring are the harvests of this world and good deeds are the harvest of the hereafter.

The following are the qualities of a gentleman:

1. Generosity
2. Suppression of anger
3. Forbearance of other's faults and misgivings
4. Pursuance of knowledge and endurance.

All are pleased with the death of the evil-minded.

When two persons abuse each other, it is the meaner of the two, who overcomes, and when two persons quarrel with each other, it is the ruder of the two, who has the upper hand.

He, who knocks at a particular door and tries constantly to enter into it, does certainly enter into it someday.

Aek Risq Woh Haai jiskay Peechhay Tum Jatay Ho Aur Aek Risq Woh Haai Jo Khood Chal Kar Tumharay Pass Aa-ta Haai.

One Risq, the sustenance or the daily bread is that in whose pursuit you go and one Risq is that which comes walking to you on its own feet.

Maula Ali says, make your character so exemplary that the Risq comes looking for you. The sustenance shows degrees of respectabilities in its honours to the recipient. It is continuously responding to match to many virtues of the recipient. And our lives be sacrificed on the ethical utterances of Maula Ali; what strategies he states in a collection of a few words.

I am constrained to quote my example here, to state of the glory and the truth statement of this Hadith.

I am a writer who never went to any school of learning to learn to write. But I write books and I am earning appreciation and monitory remunerations. And this Risq with its duality in bestowals has come walking on its own feet. My only contribution has been my hard work.

20

Friends from the Facebook

Early in 2011, two friends appeared on the Facebook, Praveen Singh and Kajal Nandini. I began monologue with them and did that as and when I could. This occupation continued for one year and more. They never replied back, except on two or three occasions in short replies. But each time they read my poetic overture which I sent in couplet and quatrain form.

Their silent role amused me, so I continued writing to them, saying verses extempore then and there. This was a rewarding bonanza from them to me, as gradually I was turning myself into a poet on their no reply.

Later Praveen Singh appeared with his portrait on his wall. He was a well-mannered young man and Kajal Nandini was a quite pleasant lady. Later she adopted the profile of a cute Scottish doll on her wall. And I never failed not to admire her silence and expressed these in my monologue. I have said some hilarious couplets addressing Praveen Singh, and Kajal Nandani. Only specimen of the monologue held with these charming friends is presented here, much of which cannot be produced for want of space in this small book:

 *Praveen Singh*

7 August 2011
Koee Poochhay Pyam-e Mohabbat Kidhar Gaya Haai
Praveen Singh Jidhar Gaya Haai Udhar Gaya Haai
If someone asks where the message of love is gone
Where Praveen Singh is gone, there it is gone.

4 August
Pyam Koee Mohabbat Ka Na Aaj Aaya Haai
Praveen Singh Tum Nay Bhi Hamein Ghumaya Haai.
No message of love has come today (from anywhere)
Praveen Singh you also have given a slip to me.

2 August
Pyam Aek Aur Mohabbat Ka Aaj Aaya Haai
Praveen Singh Dagh-o Dhakka Bus Tum Nay Lagaya Haai
One more message of love has come today
Praveen Singh you only have smeared me and shoved me.

19 July
Pyam Aur Mohabbat Ka Aek Aaya Haai
Praveen Singh Jee Tumhara He Bus Ganvaya Haai.
One more message of love has come (today)
Praveen Singh Jee yours only, I have lost.

23 August
Praveen Singh Tum Kidhar Gaya Haai
Jhoala Khali Haai Tumhara Jawab Kahan Ghusa Haai

Praveen Singh where are you gone
The bag is empty where your answer has holed in.

25 August
Mohabbat Bardi Ghun-ghoar Ghata Haai
Praveen Singh Chhupay Baaithay Raho Juldi Bhi Kya Haai
Love is enormous, pitch cloudy sky
Praveen Singh keep sitting hidden why hurry you.

27 August
Khatam Ab Ho Gaee Sari Kahani
Mohabbat Ki Rawani Taraddud Ki Zubani
The entire story has for good finished now
The flow of love through the tongue of hesitation.

27 August
Praveen Singh Tum Apna Profile Badal Dalo
Kala Aadmi Naheen Gora Aadmi Dalo.
Praveen Singh you change your profile
Not black man but post a man that is white.

29 August
Praveen Singh Khood Ko Dhakka Lagao
Engine stall Haai Isko Ghar Ghar Karao
Praveen Singh, push and push yourself
Engine that is stalled, make it do Ghar Ghar.

1 September
Praveen Singh Tumhari Baat Nirali
Khali Khooli Dosti Nikaali
Praveen Singh your way is incomparable
Created friendship of no purpose, no use.

2 September
Praveen Singh Yar Toba Karo
Bhagwan Ki Qasam Yar Baat Karo
Praveen Singh my friend do start penitence
By God my mate, make conversation.

5 September
Praveen Singh Ajab Si Dhithda-ee Haai
Saari Khuda-ee Mein Tumnay Laga-ee Haai.
Praveen Singh this is strange stubbornness
In the entire Kingdom of God you have incrusted.

7 September
Praveen Singh Tumhara Jawab Naheen
Bhagtay Raehtay Ho Sans Lo Baat Karo
Praveen Singh you have no one like you
You keep running take a breath and talk to me.

19 September
Praveen Singh what is the matter
Breeze, sun, moon, couplets don't matter?

18 September
Praveen Singh Ji we are friends
You quite, me blabbering old friend.

6 September
Kaun Kahta Haai Tum Mukarram Naheen
Baat Mano Qabil! Bano Bhalay Manus Tum
Apni Roodad Tum Sunao Zara
Hans Kay Bolo Yahee Saughat, Aai Haan

Who says you are not revered

Do listen competent you become a good man
Tell something of your story
Speak pleasantly this is the rare gift, Oh yes.

19 September
Praveen Singh Jee why you not speak
Violate your vow; speak!

20 September
Praveen Singh you are my friend
You send me no reply why my friend?

27 September
Praveen Singh Kab Bologay?
Jaldi Karo Kya Sathh Chhordo Gay?
Praveen Singh when will you speak?
Do hurry! What? Will you abandon togetherness?

29 September
Praveen Singh Tum Nay Bhang Pe Daali Haai
Hilata Dulata Hoon Hiltay Dultay Naheen
Praveen Singh you have drunk Indian hemp
I shake and jolt you, still you make no movement.

5 October
Praveen Singh Tum Nay Hud Kar Dali Haai
Jawab Nadarad Sirf Shakl Dikhla Dali Haai
Praveen Singh you have made limit in excess
Answer absent just showing face you put to be seen.

13 October
Praveen Singh Yar Kuchh Toe Bolo
Dam Saadh Kay Baaithay Ho Ghatar Goon Hi Karo

Praveen Singh my mate do speak something!
You are sitting drawing your breath, do if nothing
Ghatar Ghoon.

13 October
Praveen Singh Jee Bardi Sakht Ghardi Aayee Haai
Tum Nay Aur Kajal Nandani nay Jawab Na Deynay Ki Qasam Khaee haai
Praveen Singh Jee this a moment of extreme trial
You and Kajal Nandini have vowed to eat up reply.

13 November at 13:08 Report
SIR HOWS UR LIFE GOING
Sent from mobile phone.

13 November
Kya Poochhtay Ho Hall Mera Dosto Meray
Khadday Mein Chhoard Daord Rahay Ho Bahar Mein
What are you asking of my condition my friends
Leaving me in the ditch you are running in the spring.

15 November
Praveen Singh Tum Nay Phir Goal Kiya
Phuljhardi Chhord Ker Gham Oondale Diya
Praveen Singh again you have duped
After cracking firework, thrown grief in the mood.

16 November
Praveen Singh Tum Nay Khota Dekha Haai
Do Kan Char Paon Hum Say Mota Haai
Praveen Singh have you seen an ass
He has two ears four legs, he is fatter than us.

18 November
Praveen Singh Naya Gurd Khao
Jan Banti Haai Toe Mujhko Batao
Praveen Singh eat new lump of raw sugar (Gurd)
If you gain vitality then you tell me for sure.

20 November at 09:37
Praveen Singh Tum Thargatwa Jao
Wahan Maain Ghooma Phira Hoon Haal Batao
Praveen Singh you go to Thargatwa (Mountain near Chakia)
I have visited it around you tell how it is now.

22 November at 18:24
Praveen Singh Qurani Aayat Pardho
Daan Pun Karo Allah Walay Bano
Praveen Singh go and read the verses of Quran
Make charity do good work, become of God.

 *Sayed Athar Husain*

23 November at 22:20
Praveen Singh Tum Raja Bhog Ka Nirmay Kar Kay Ashpat Mein Kuroadh wibhash Kartay Rahna. Kathdin Way Nishchit Paryag Karkay Uddhyan Karna. Samajh Samajh Karna.

(This nonsense was written to look like Vedic words of a Pundit and attract Praveen Singh's attention).

Ok sir u can ask anything of India from me I will definitely help u……………………Praveen

Saying of Hazrat Ali A.S.:

A fluent speech is that which can be easily uttered by the tongue and not hard to hear (one free from affectation and artificiality).

 *Kajal Nandini*

Hello, Kajal Nandini

05 August 2011
Achchay Achchoan Kay Hosh Urd Jaein
Fakhtaein Bhatak Bhatak Jaein
Sound and good of thinking slump and lose senses
Doves get lost and wander without direction.

05 August at 20:29
Titliyan Urdein Her Dum
Mendhkian Karein Ghatar Gham, Ghatar Gham.
The butterflies volunteer flying all the time
The female of frogs doing Ghatar Gham, Ghatar Gham.

06 August at 12:09
Chalk Chauband, Hoashdaar, Bay Hoash
Makhoal, Hansi, Daghadam, Daghadam.

Active, alert, vigilant, conscious, unconscious
Jest, joke, Daghadam, Daghadam.

13 August at 23:49
Khuda Hafiz, Qadar Dani, Mohabbat, Khak Nasheeni
Saughat-e Face Book Haai Jisay Toom Karti Naheen
Good bye then! Due regard, love, humility
This is a present of Face Book you not doing.

18 August at 23:29
Kajal Nandani Tumhara Kajal Kahan Haai
Aankh Bay Kajal Haai Neechay Aankh Garda Haai
Kajal Nandini where your lamp-black eyeliner is
Eye is without eyeliner and fixed downward on floor.

18 August at 23:32
Chashmay Aahoo Haai Tumhari Aankh
Shaher Aaee Haai Dasht-o Jhaardi say
Your eyes are eyes of the deer
Which have come to the city from desert and bush.

19 August at 17:07
Raaz Kya Haai Keh Tum Bolti Naheen
Butd Ho Toom Ya Koee Jinnatni
What the secret is you do not speak?
You are a statue or female Jinn.

25 August at 01:15
Sawan Gaya Bahar Aaee, Bahar Gaee Sardi Aaee
Kajal, Tumhari Baat Na Badli Na Tum Badal Paee
Sawan (July) went spring came, spring went winter came
Kajal, neither your way changed nor you could change.

27 August at 07:03
Khatam Ab Ho Gaee Sari Kahani
Mohabbat Ki Rawani Taraddud Ki Zubani
The entire story now finished
The out flow of love through the tongue of reservation.

29 August at 16:47
Kab Ko Bologee Yar kuchh Bolo
Praveen Singh Tak Aek Bar Bola Haai
When will you speak O mate speak something
Praveen Singh even has spoken once.

29 August at 16:51
Meray Ustad Tum Dono Ho
Sha-ayree Tum Say Maain Nay Seekha Haai
My teacher you two are
I have learnt poetry from you two.

03 September at 00:04
Kash Kuchh Toe Kaeh Diya Hota
Bali Kajal Na Honay Say Hona Hota
Wish you had said something
Tender Kajal something was better than nothing.

'Hi' from Kajal Nandini

05 September at 18:17
Begum Bholi Bardi Pyari Suno
Dum Khood Ho-kay Na Baaitho Jhat Uttho Jhat Uttho.
Begum innocent very dear listen
Don't sit motionless stunt, stand at once stand at once?

06 September at 22:58
Apni Bhagti Karo Bhagtan Say
Bhaag Bhagan Kay Khola-o Bhagwun Say
Get your worship done by the worshippers
Get fortune opened of the fortunate by the Godly.

13 September at 12:46
Kajal Tumhari Dosti Bardhti Chalee Gaee
Paehlay Anda Thee Phir Murghee Bun Gaee
Kurd, Kurd Karnay Lagee Anday Daar Ho Gaee
Daekhtay Hi Daekhtay Bachchay Daar Ho Gaee

Kajal your friendship kept growing
First it was egg then it became grown hen
Kurd, Kurd it started doing, egg laying it became.
Without passing much time baby mother it became

14 September at 11:22
Kajal Nandini Agar Tum Na Hoti
Sha-ayree Na Hoti Ta-ey-unnat Na Hoti
Kajal Nandini if you were not there
Poetry I would do naught, turning over to it will be naught.

16 September at 11:42
Mohabbat Kay Haain Jo Andaz Niralay
Tumhari Qasam Bhagat Bhagtoot Bhagay
Love which has such strange ways
By Joe, ascetic will run away from it like mad.

16 September at 12:16
Tum Ko Andaza Gar Naheen Mera
Mujh Ko Andaza Khood Naheen Mera

If you have no guess of me
I have no estimate myself of me.

16 September at 12:21
Gurd Gurdata Hoon Shaeroan Ki Tareh
Jan Ganwata Hoon Kakrdoan Ki Tareh
I coo like poets
Squander myself as a fast running stag.

(Glossary: *Kakrda* is a deer like *Sanbhar* which runs *Bagtoot* – fast).

19 September at 23:06
Kajal Nandini get up and go
Don't go, don't go, yes go.

20 September at 22:52
Kajal Nandini it's dumb
If you don't reply and keep mum.

01 October at 20:15
You are no doubt tucked to stoniness
Nothing works to lure you to suaveness.

05 October at 23:59
Kajal Nandini Bardi Sakht Gha-rdee Aa-ee Haai
Tum Nay Aur Praveen Singh Nay Jawab Na Deynay Ki Qasam Khaee Haai
Kajal Nandini, hour of extreme difficulty has arrived
You and Praveen Singh have vowed not to reply.

13 October at 21:55
Kajal Nandini you are European

Indian, Persian, Arabian or a Zartushtian?

16 October at 22:05
Kajal Nandini stay in the house
There is frost outside and you slight.

18 October at 23:29
Kajal Nandini tell me if you smile
Or brood always and remain cradle tied?

18 October at 23:35
Kajal Nandani you are not cruel, but bore,
Never reply never own laurel and lore.

Kajal Nandini: - Replies with a 'Hello'

07 September at 23:02
Thank you, thank you Janab-e Wala
Made me yours, Yeh Kamal Kar Dala.
Thank you, thank you respected eminent
Made me yours did this wonder of wonders.

Sayings of Hazrat Ali A.S.:

Love your friend only up to a limit; because perhaps someday he may become your enemy and keep the enmity with your enemy only within a limit, it is possible someday he might become your friend.

Fear God, be it a little, and keep a veil between you and God, be it very transparent.

-:. .:-

www.ingramcontent.com/pod-product-compliance
Lightning Source LLC
Chambersburg PA
CBHW022114090426
42743CB00008B/839